100
GHOSTS

100 GHOSTS

a gallery of
harmless haunts

by Doogie Horner

QUIRK BOOKS

PHILADELPHIA

© 2013 BY DOOGIE HORNER
ALL RIGHTS RESERVED. NO PART OF
THIS BOOK MAY BE REPRODUCED IN
ANY FORM WITHOUT PERMISSION FROM
THE PUBLISHER.

LIBRARY OF CONGRESS CATALOGING IN
PUBLICATION NUMBER: 2013930160

ISBN: 978-1-59474-647-5

PRINTED IN CHINA
DESIGNED BY DOOGIE HORNER
PRODUCTION MANAGEMENT BY
    JOHN J. McGURK

QUIRK BOOKS
215 CHURCH ST.
PHILADELPHIA, PA 19106
QUIRKBOOKS.COM

10 9 8 7 6 5 4 3 2 1

I used to be scared of ghosts, until one evening I walked into my kitchen and found a spooky little guy struggling to get the lid off a jar of pickles. That's when I realized that ghosts are just like us! They get nervous at parties, love pizza, & sometimes fall asleep during long meetings.

Heck, compared to most things that go bump in the night, ghosts aren't scary at all. One night I heard some noise downstairs. I crept out of bed expecting to find a ghost making a sandwich, but instead I found a pregnant possum going into labor. Let me assure you: possums are far, far scarier than ghosts.

A ghost might ask you to solve his murder, and if you demur, the worst [redacted] he'll do is make some lamps float, or hide your toothbrush. A pregnant possum, on the other hand, will bite you, scratch you, and scatter baby possums into all the hard-to-reach corners. If you ask an exorcist to help you get rid of a possum, he'll refuse, because he knows its bite could turn him into a werehillbilly, doomed to play in a jug band & roam the bayous every full moon.

Why are people afraid of ghosts? I [redacted]k its because ghosts say "boo," & people are afraid of critcism, but [redacted] because ghosts live in graveyards and are sometimes filled with spiders.

But ghosts are just dead people, and most people are nice. Sure, there's always the occasional demon hand or electrocuted convict, but the majority of ghosts are very helpful. They can lead you to buried treasure, teach you how to use the Force, or show you the true meaning of Christmas.

I hope these spectral portraits change the way you look at the recently deceased. And don't worry, none of these ghosts are filled with spiders (although one is full of bees).

CLASSIC

1

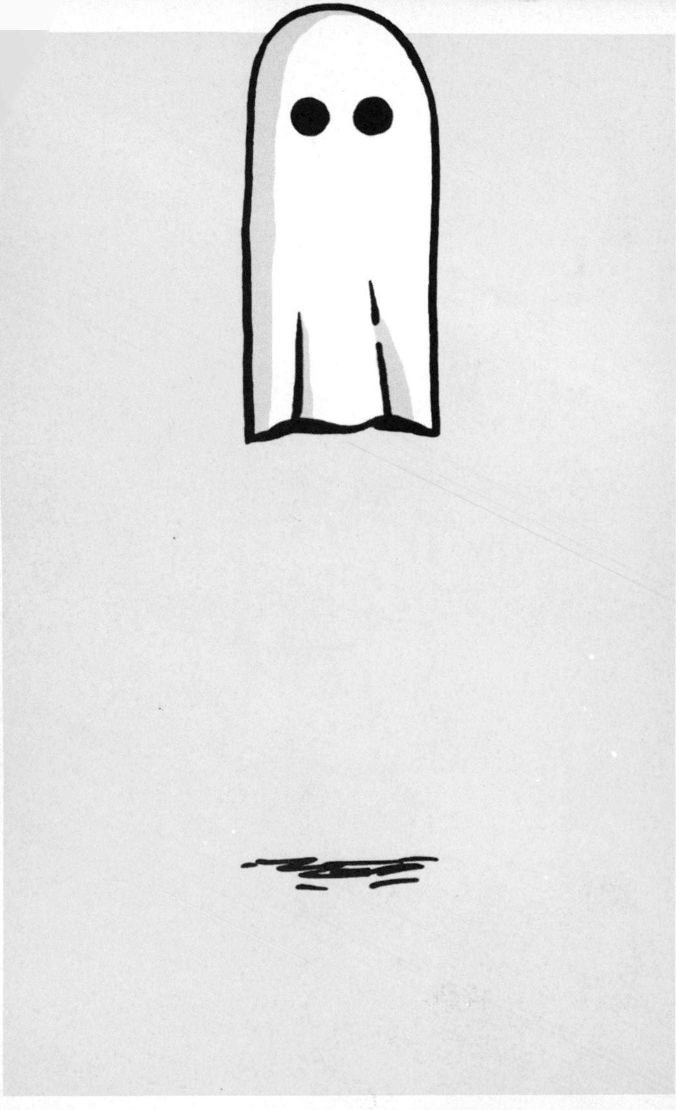

ATHLETIC

2

AFTER A BATH

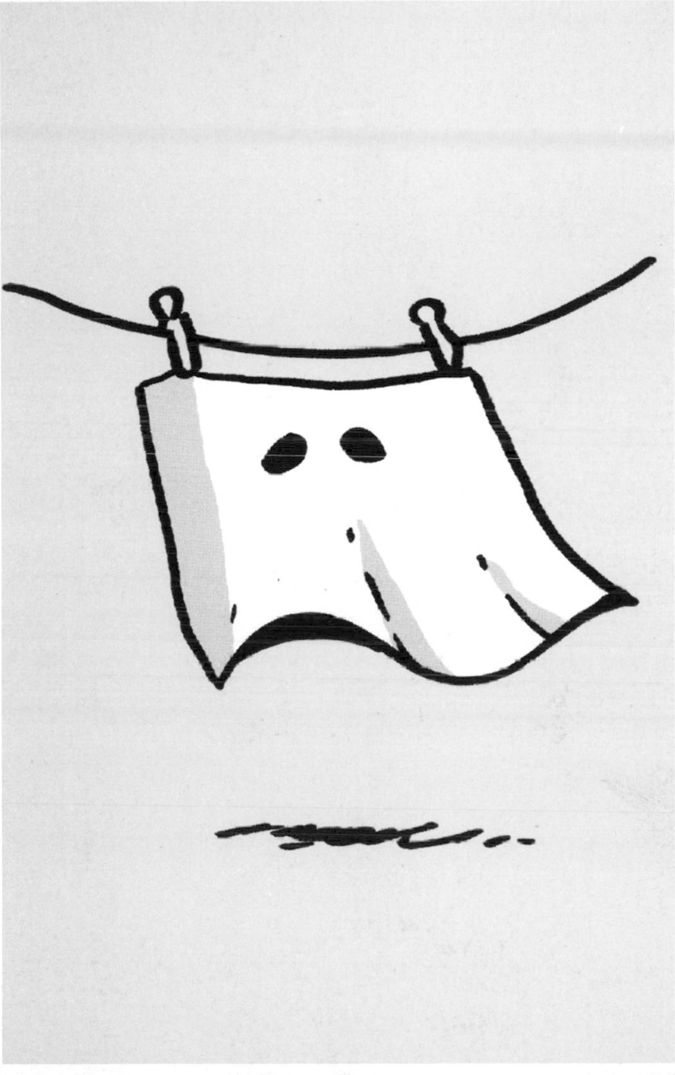

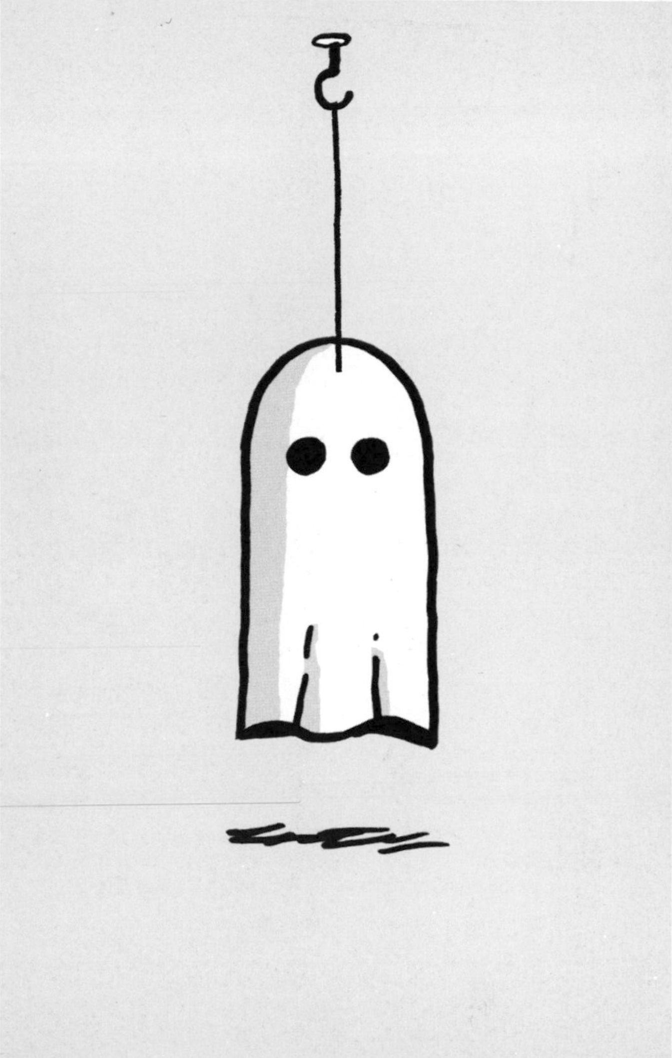

FAKE

4

SHY

5

R2-D2

6

IRONIC

7

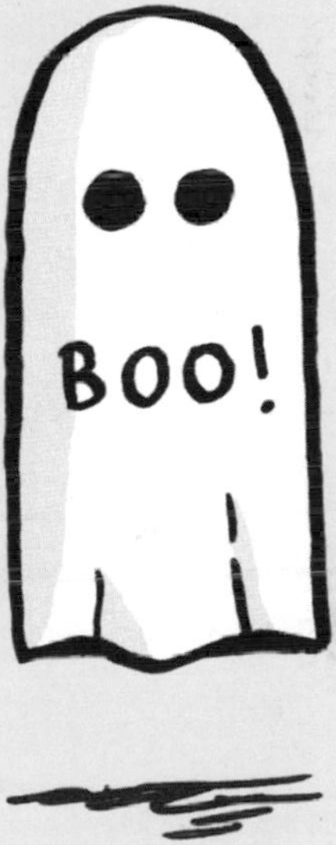
BOO!

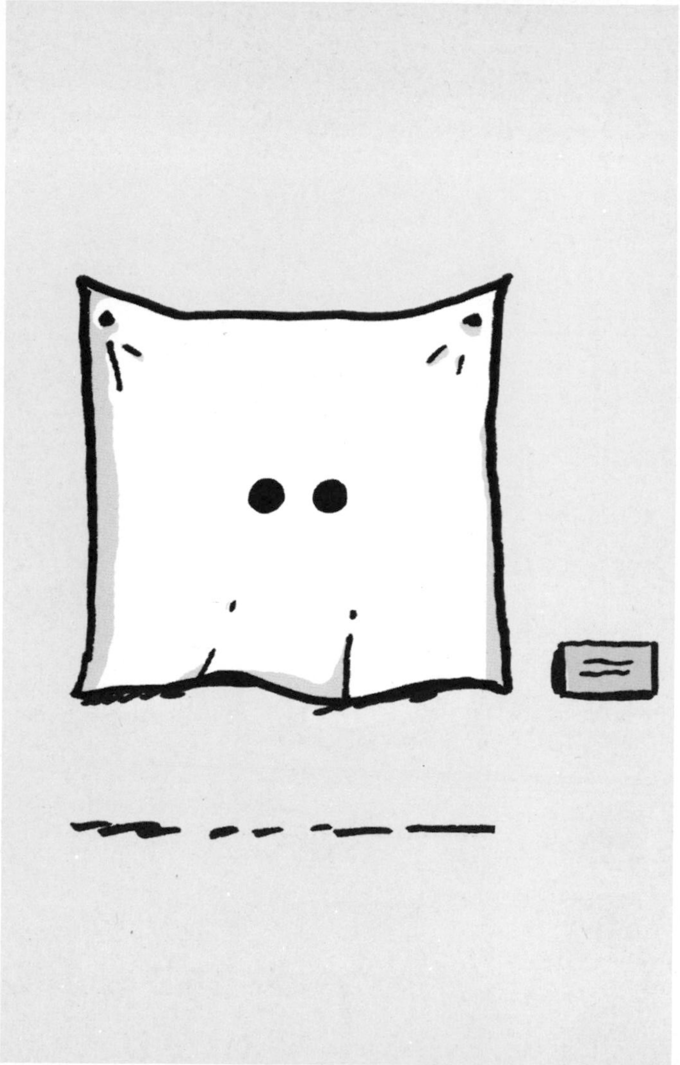

PERFORMANCE
ARTIST

8

FITTED SHEET

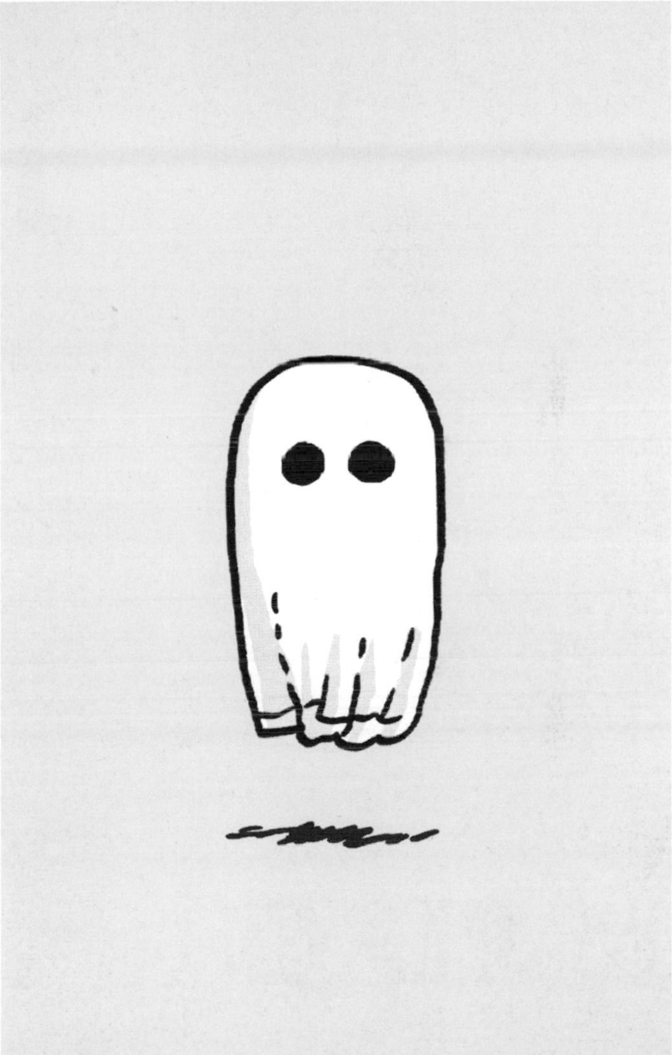

PILLOWCASE

10

LLAMA

11

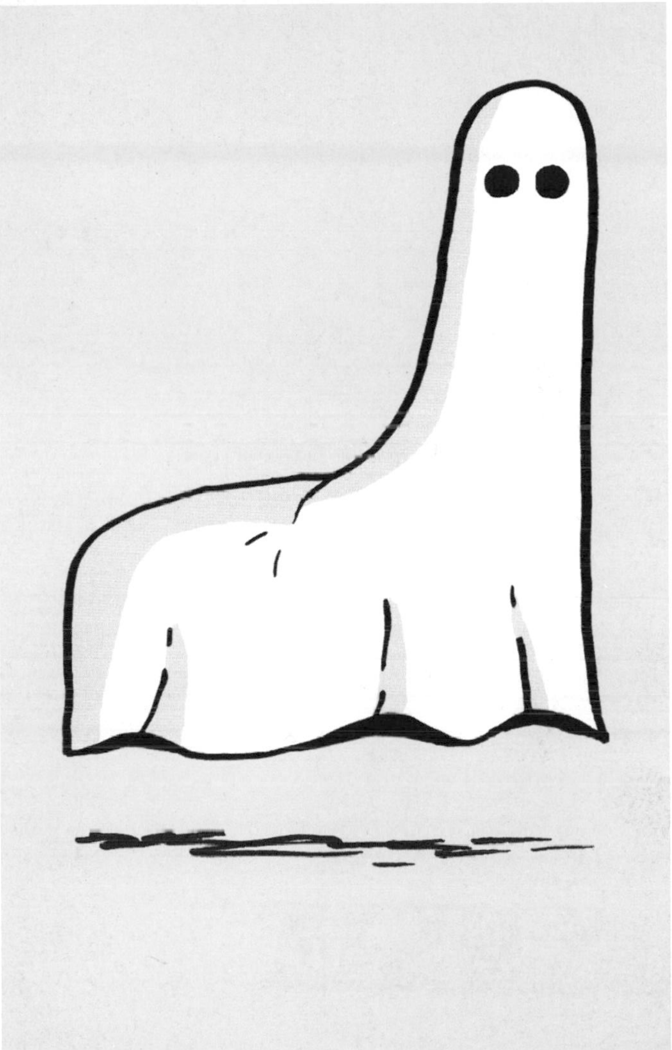

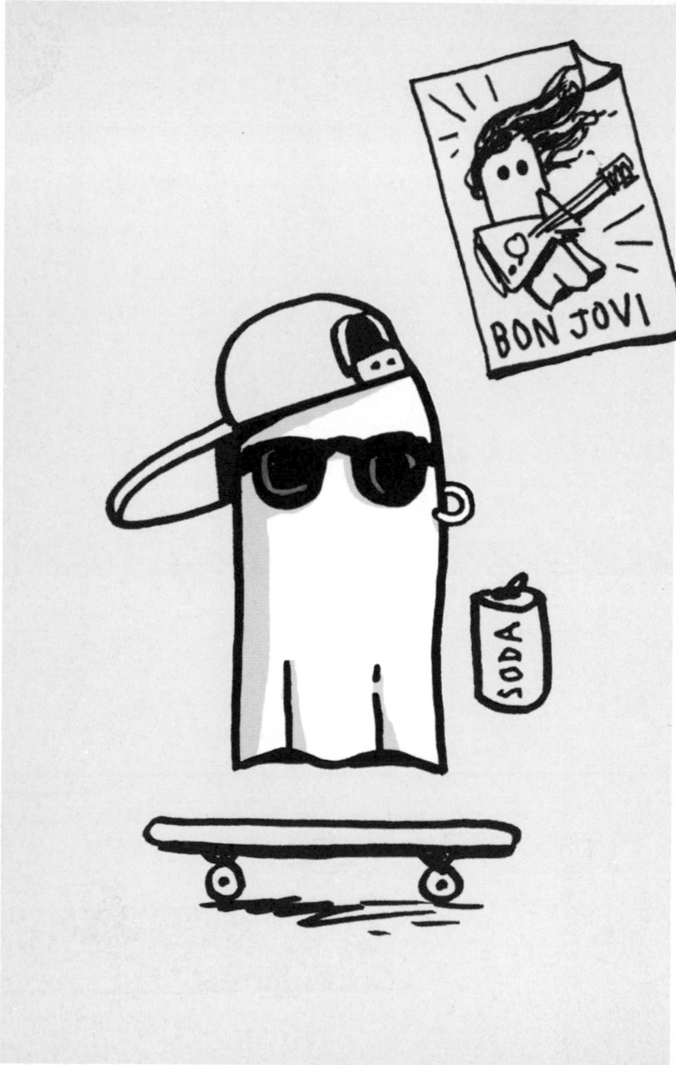
BON JOVI
SODA

RADICAL

12

NERVOUS

13

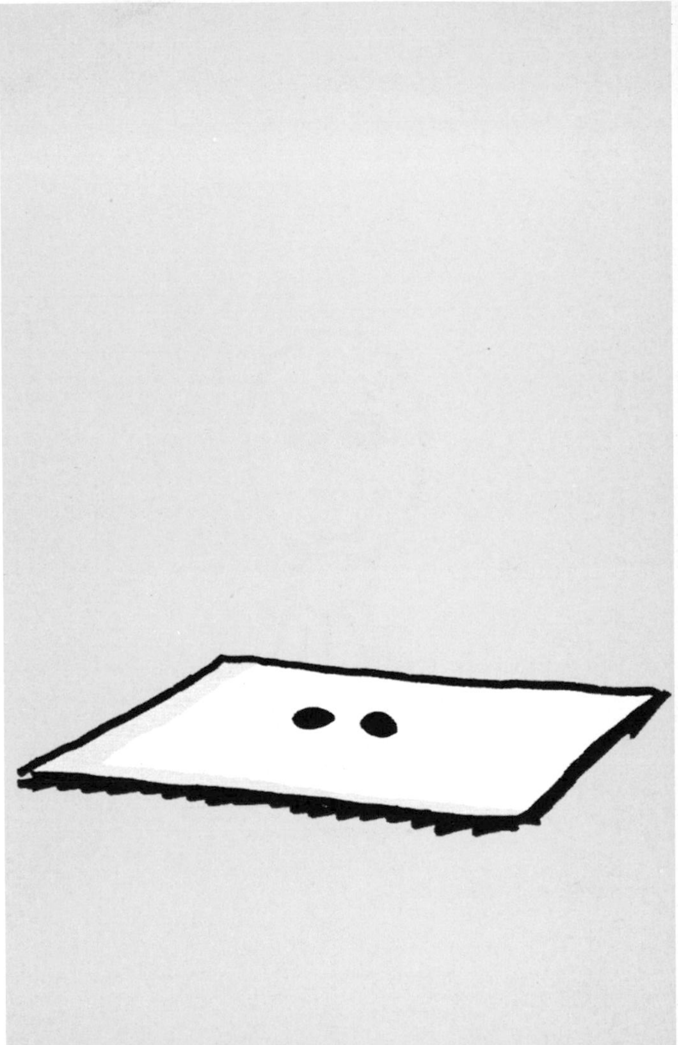

LAZY

14

SIAMESE TWINS

15

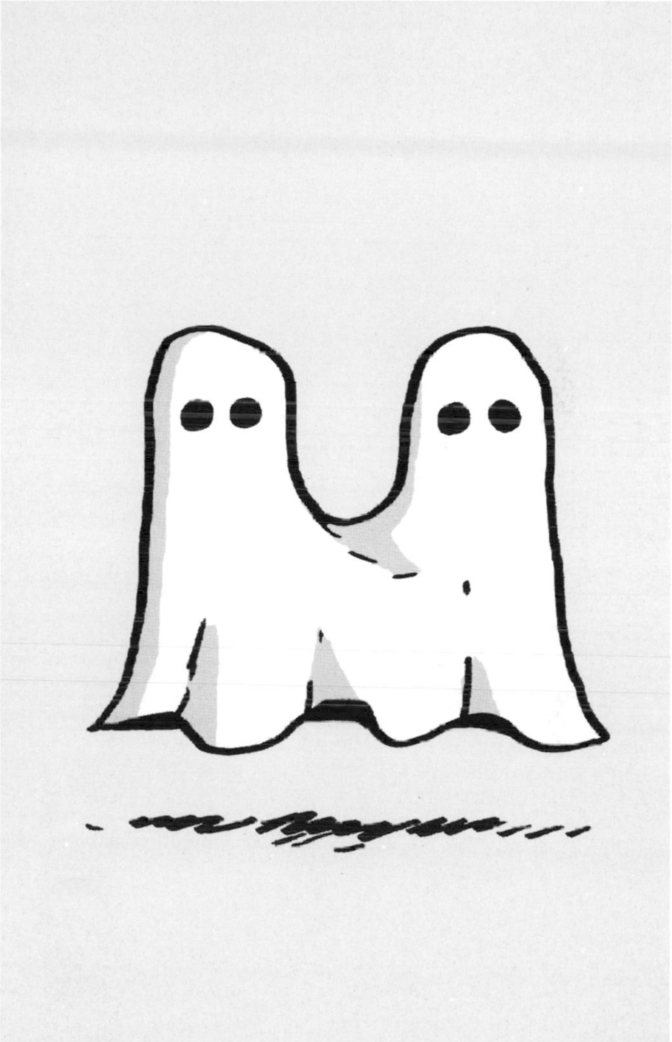

PAC-MAN

16

BIRDHOUSE

17

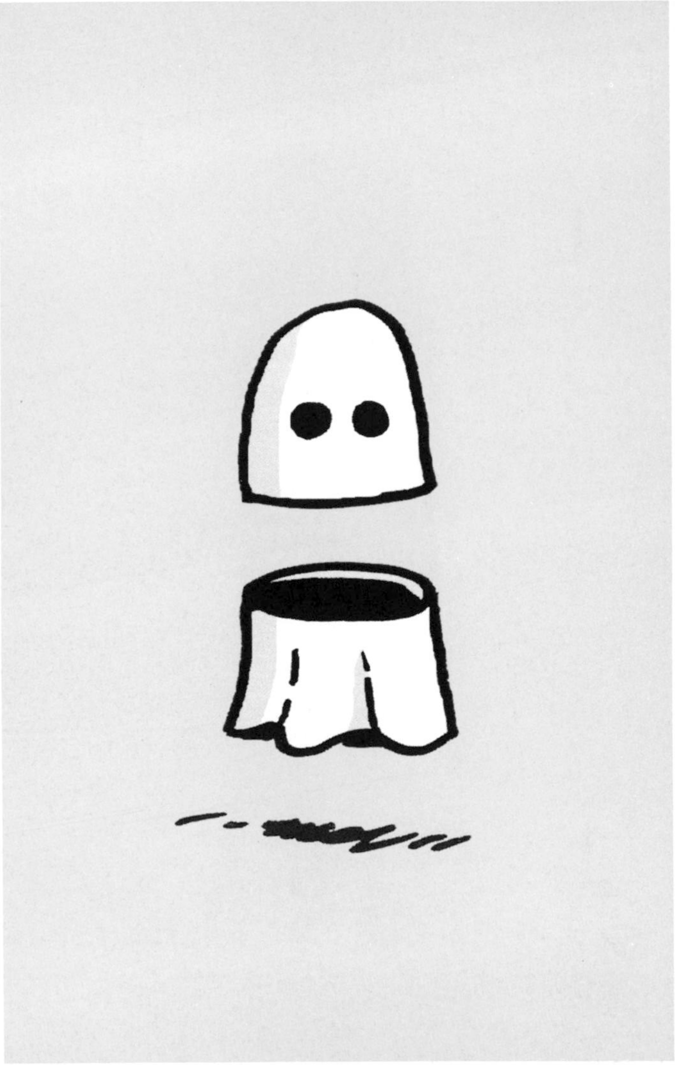

BIKINI

18

HOMEMADE

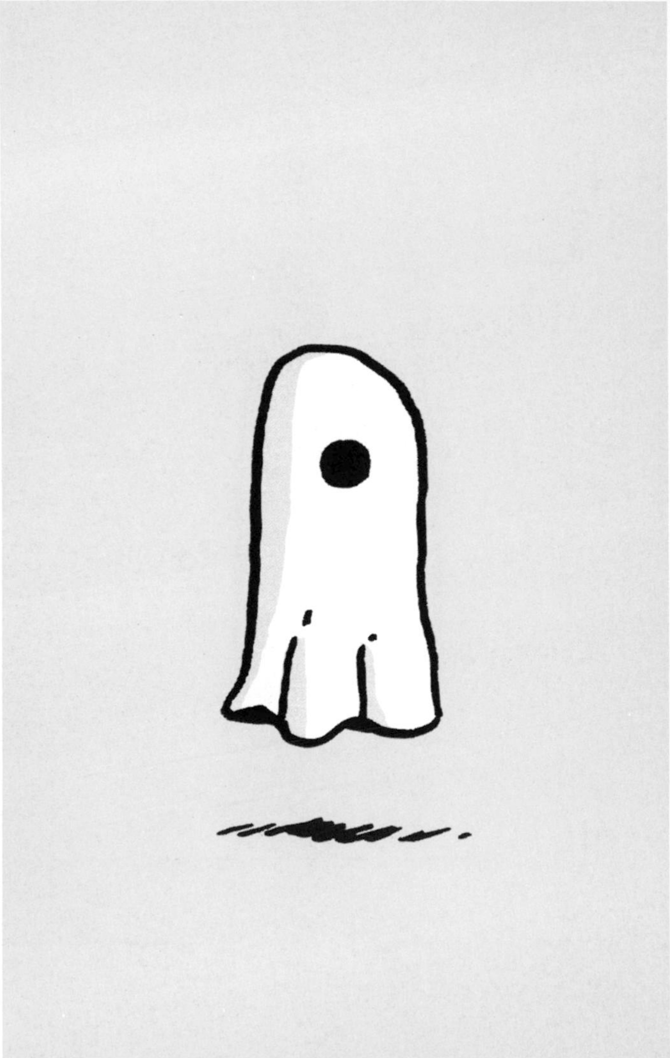

CYCLOPS
(MYTHICAL)

20

CYCLOPS
(X-MEN)

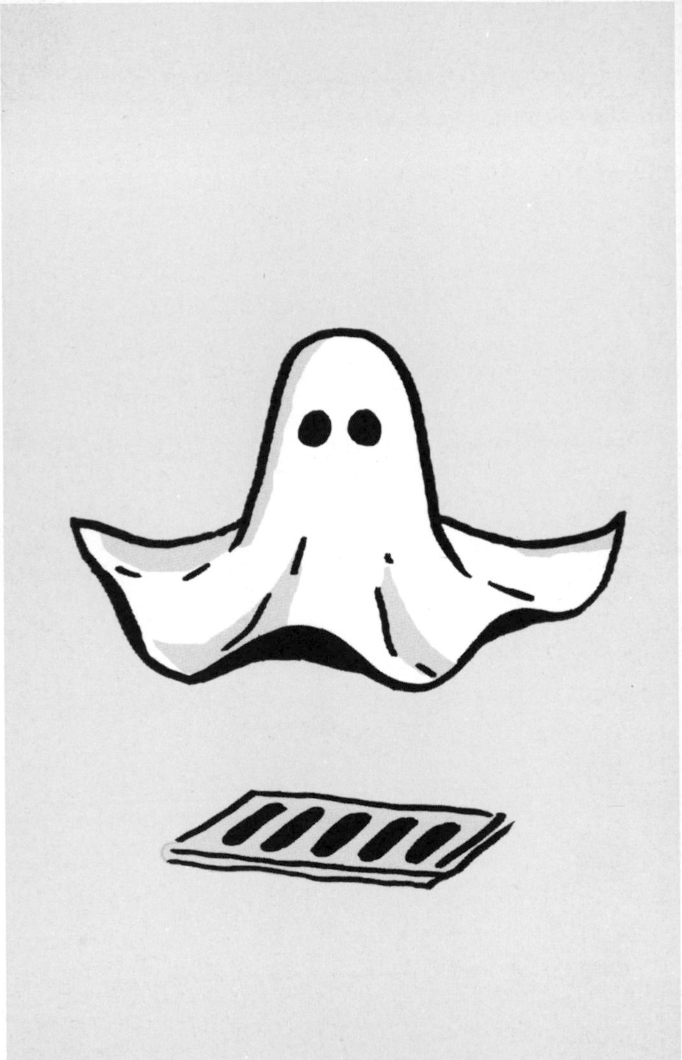

MARILYN MONROE

22

SNOWMAN

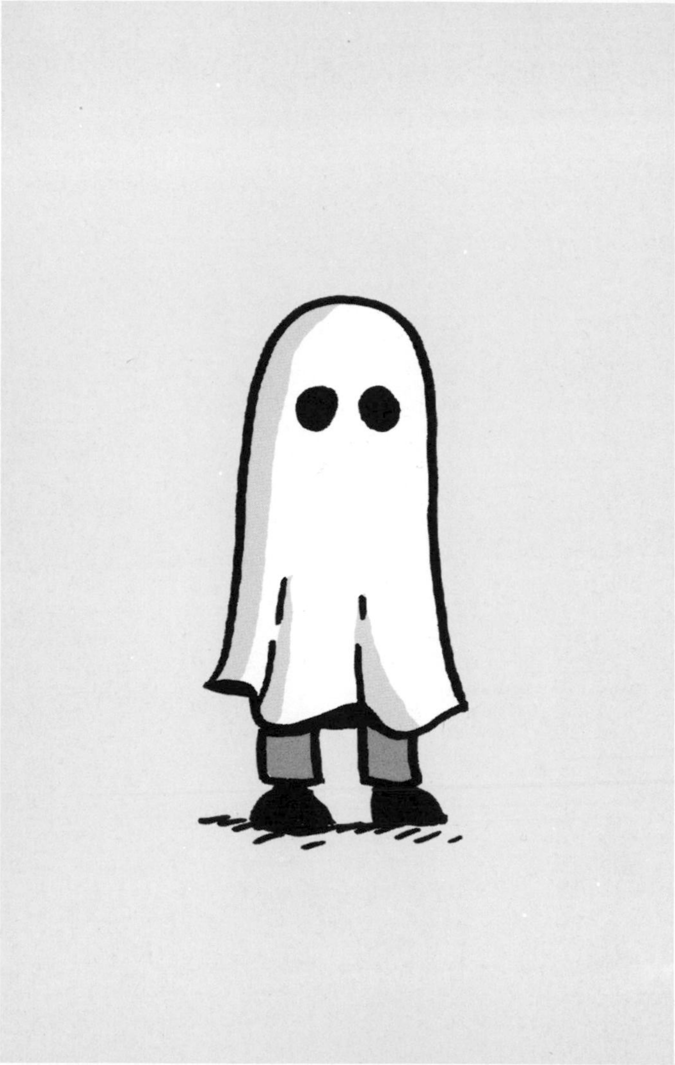

TRICK OR
TREAT

24

ACROBAT

25

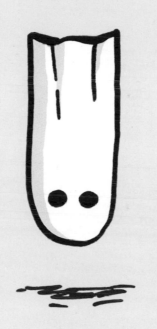

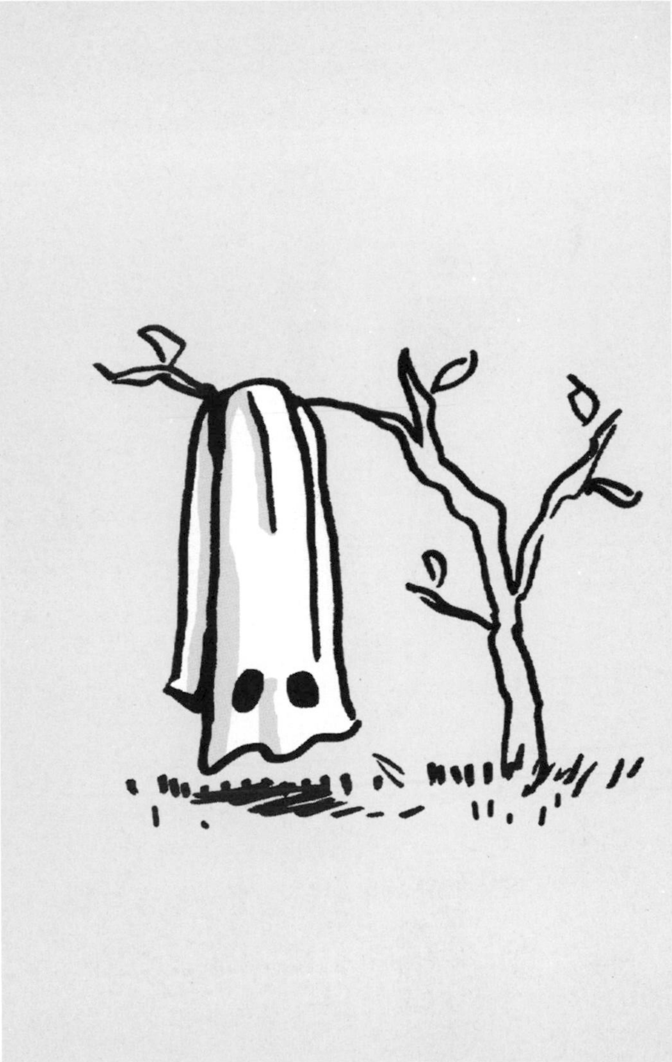

NUDIST

26

FRIENDLY

UNDERCOVER
COP

28

SURPRISED

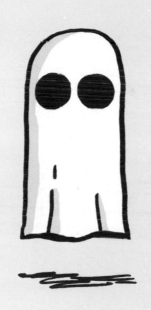

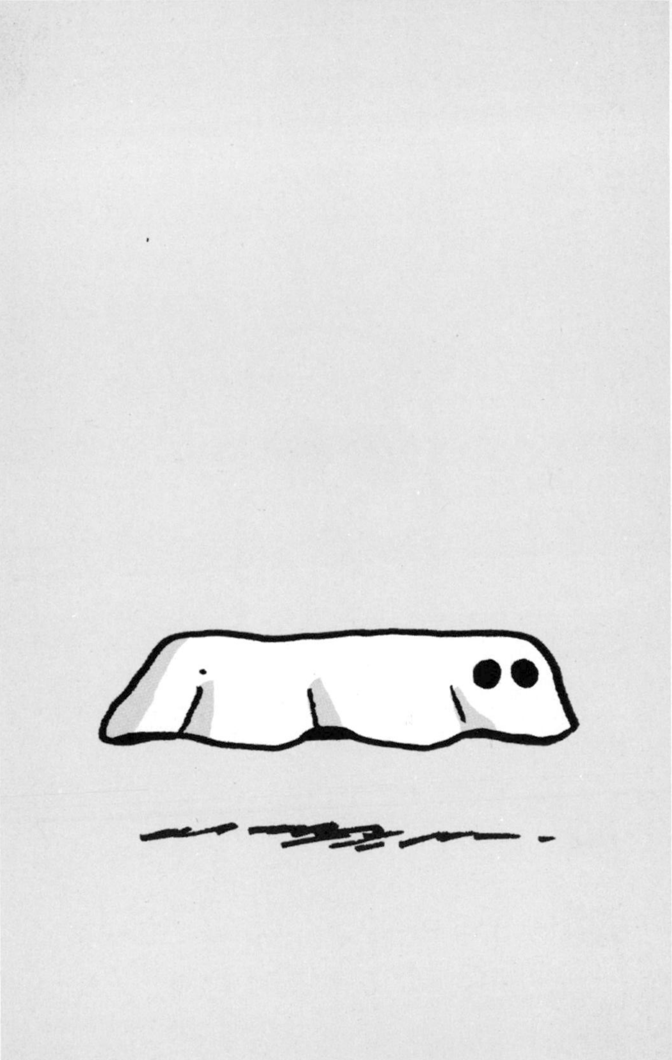

DACHSHUND

30

MINI
DACHSHUND

31

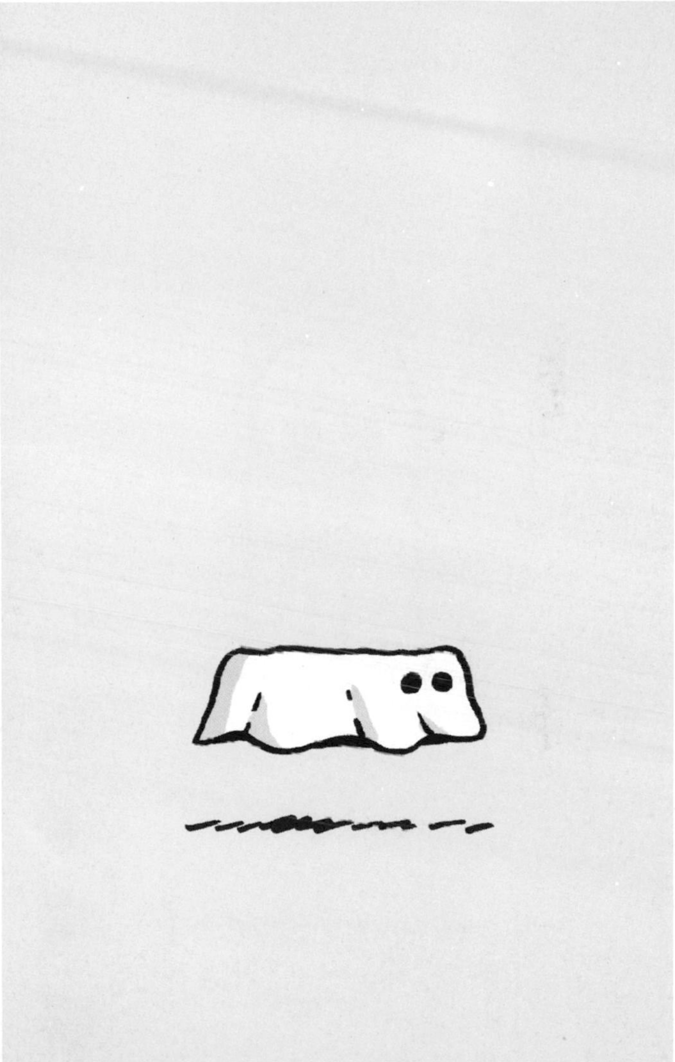

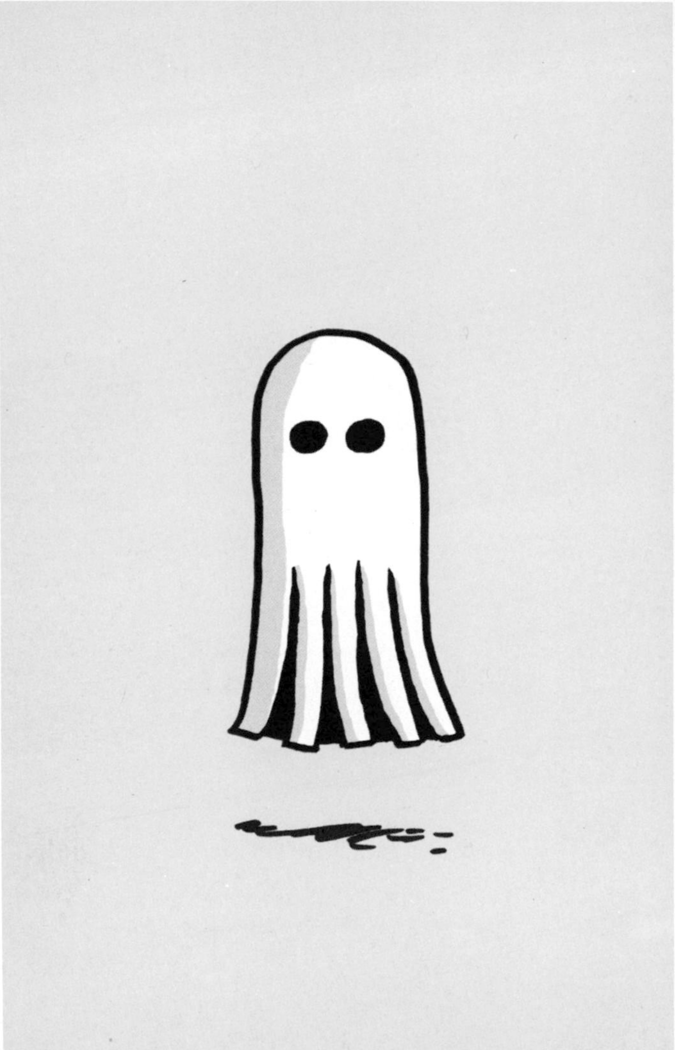

OCTOPUS

32

FAT

33

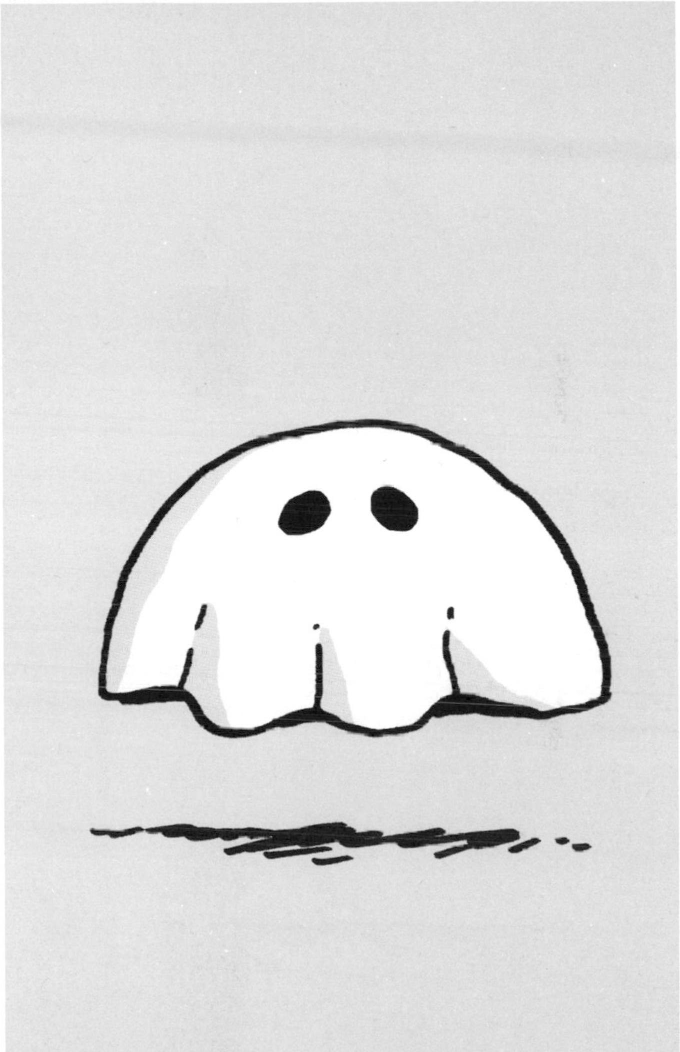

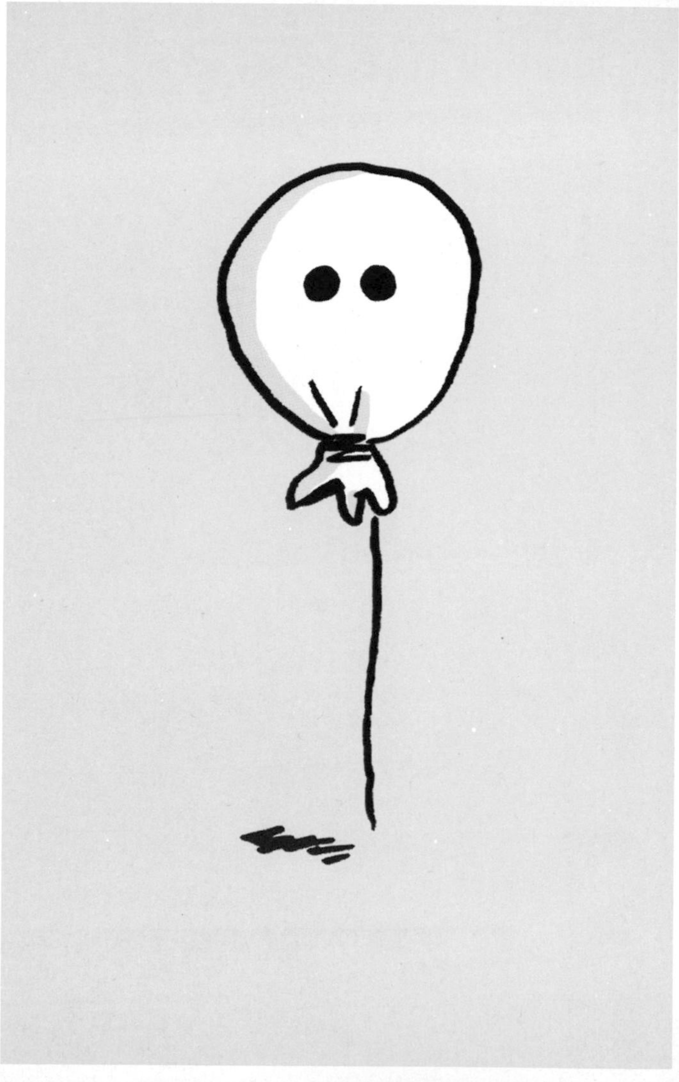

PARTY GHOST

34

EYE CHART

35

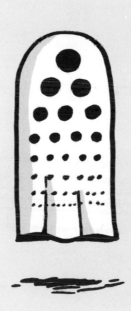

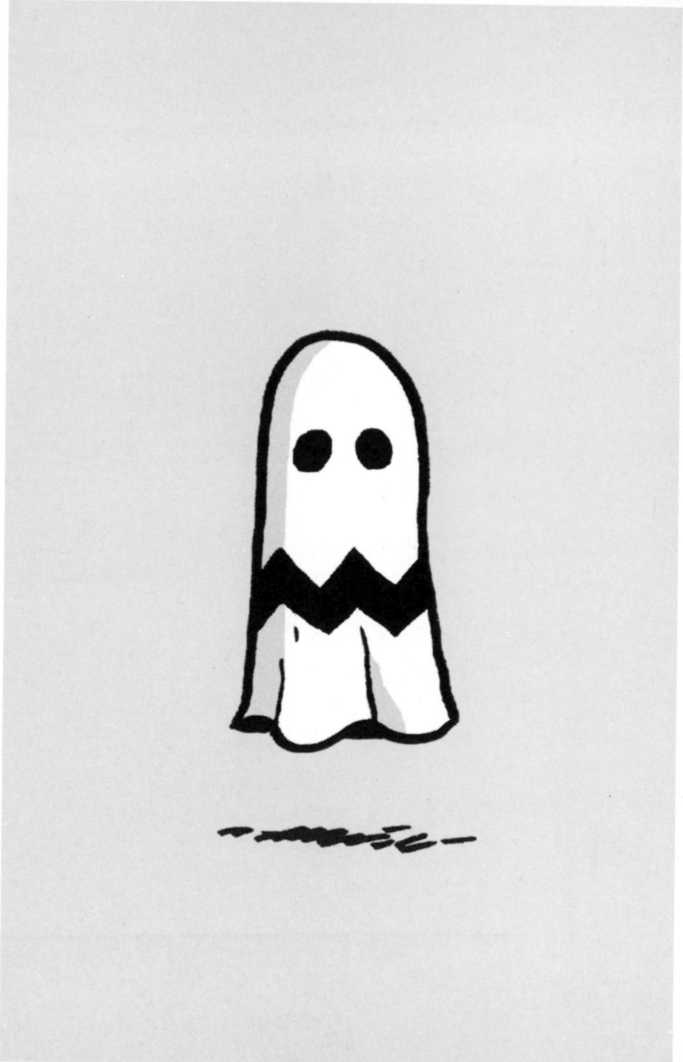

CHARLIE BROWN

IN LOVE

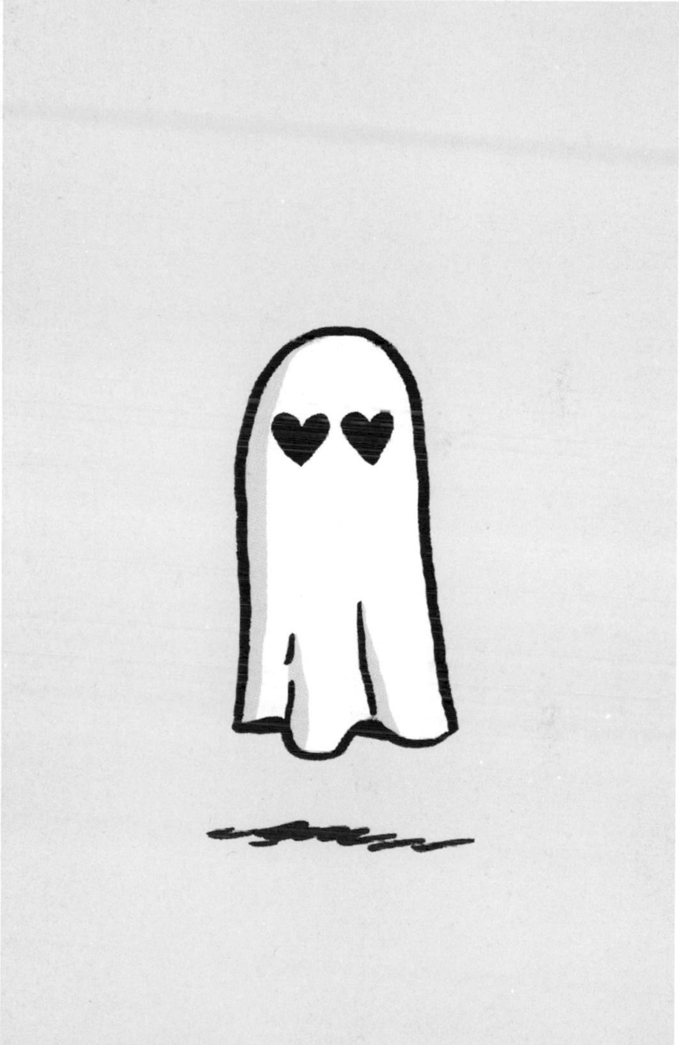

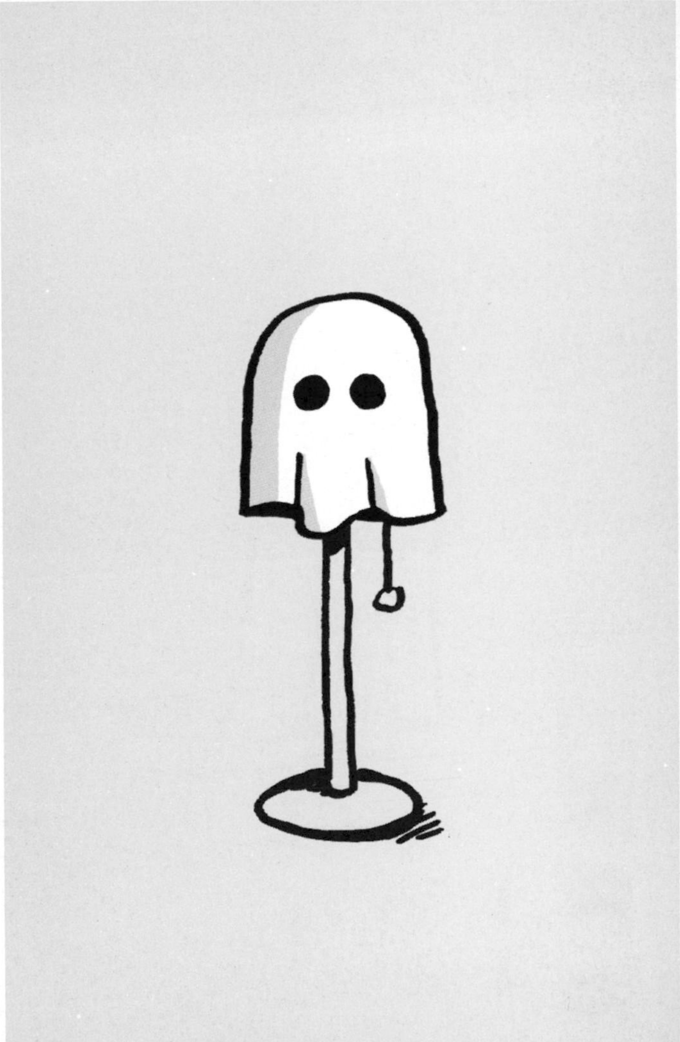

LAMP

38

STARCHED

39

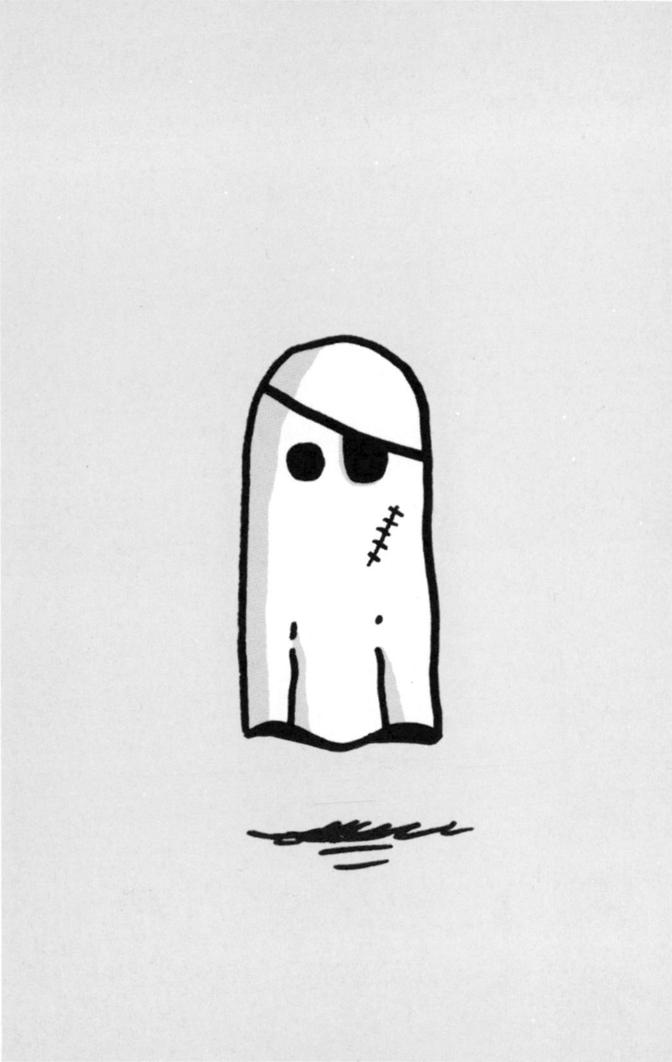

BOND VILLAIN

40

PIRATE

41

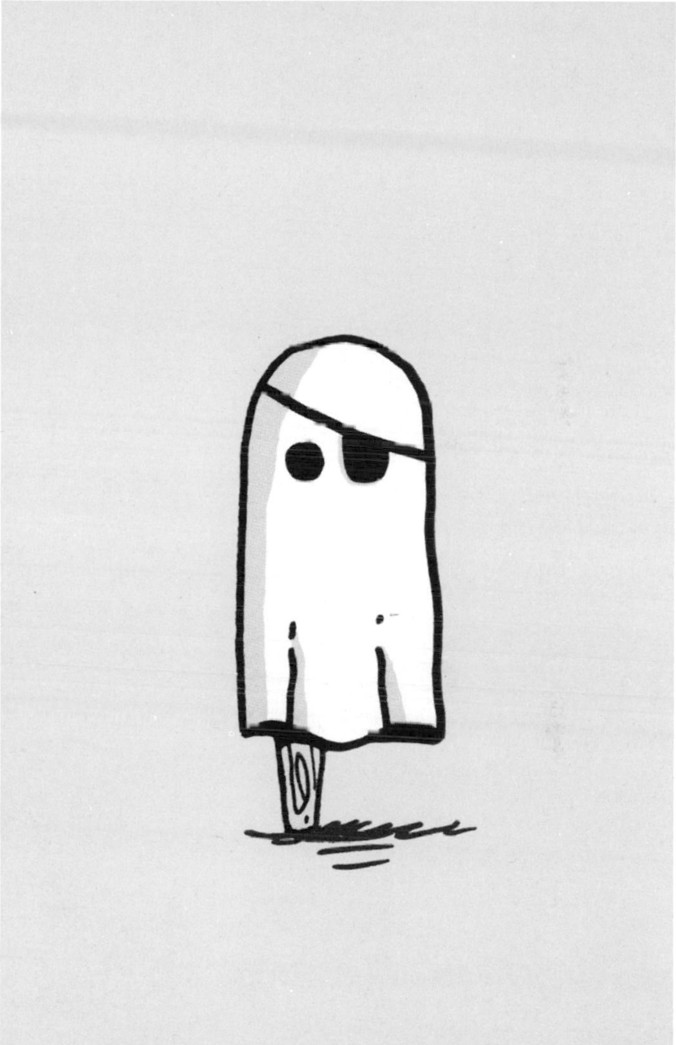

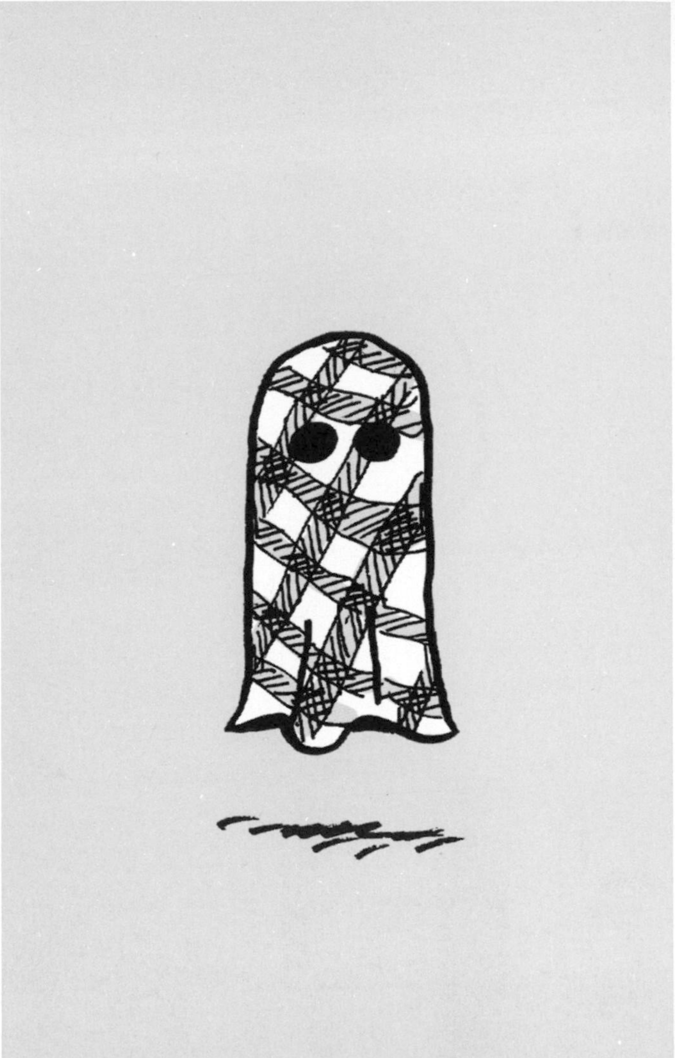

SCOTTISH

42

KING-SIZE BED

43

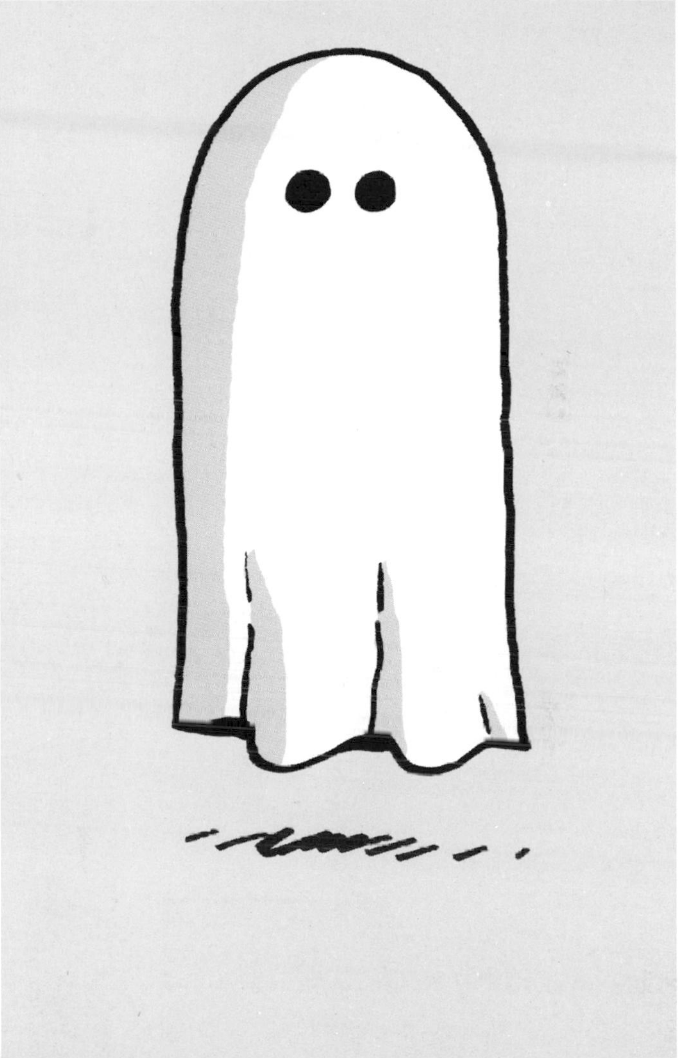

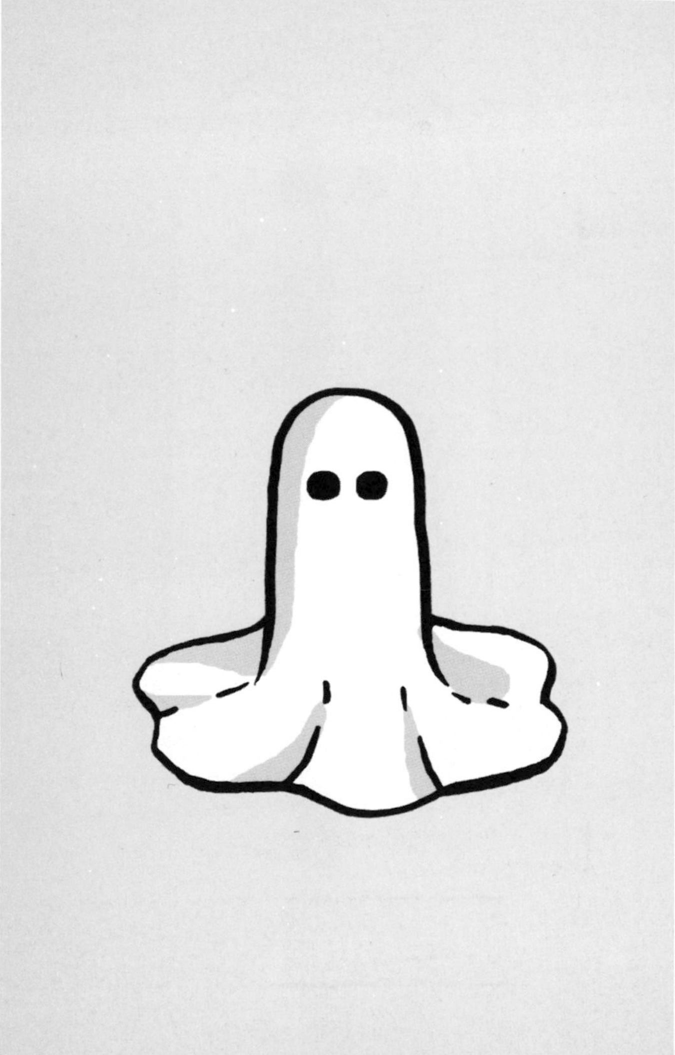

TOO SHORT

44

PREGNANT

45

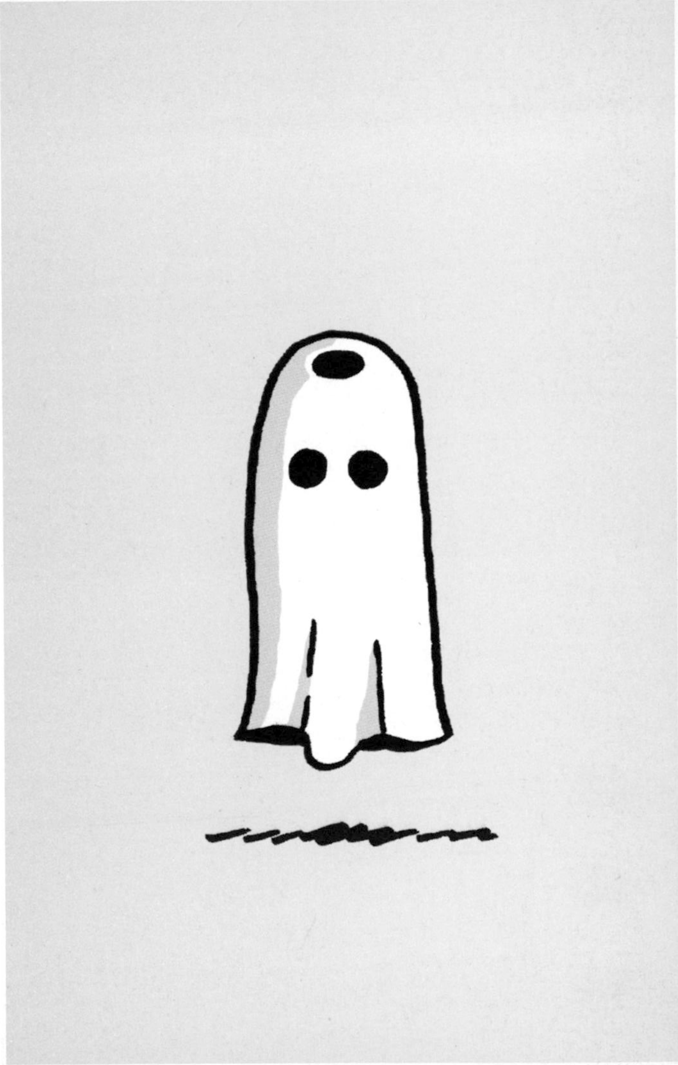

DOLPHIN

46

TWO KIDS
STANDING ON
EACH OTHER'S
SHOULDERS

47

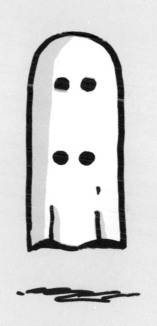

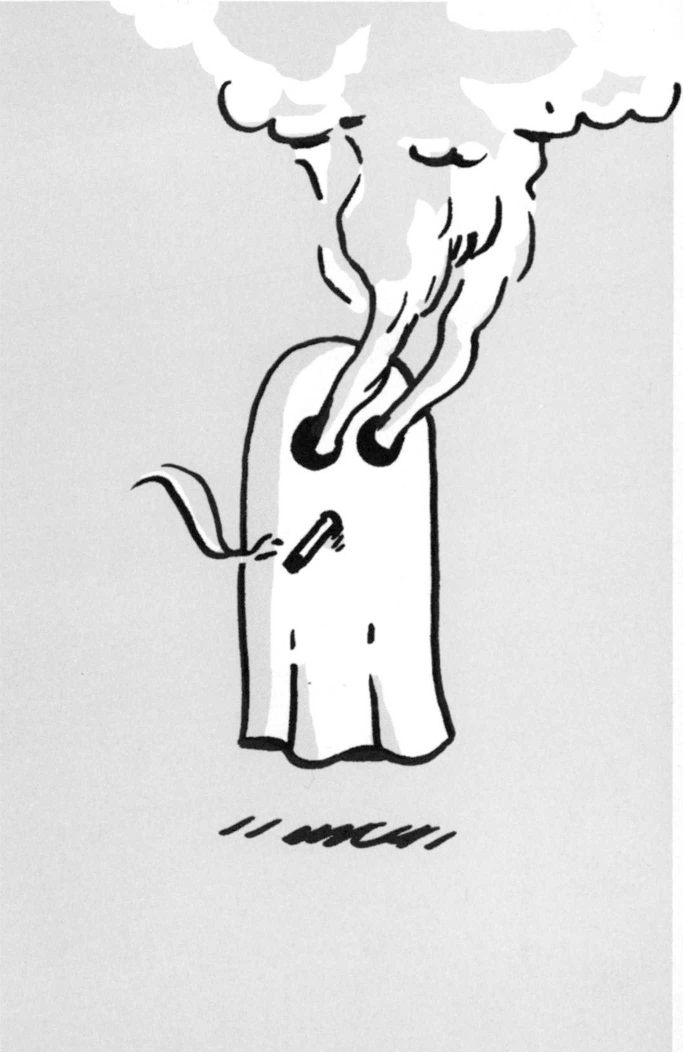

SMOKER

48

DOMINO

49

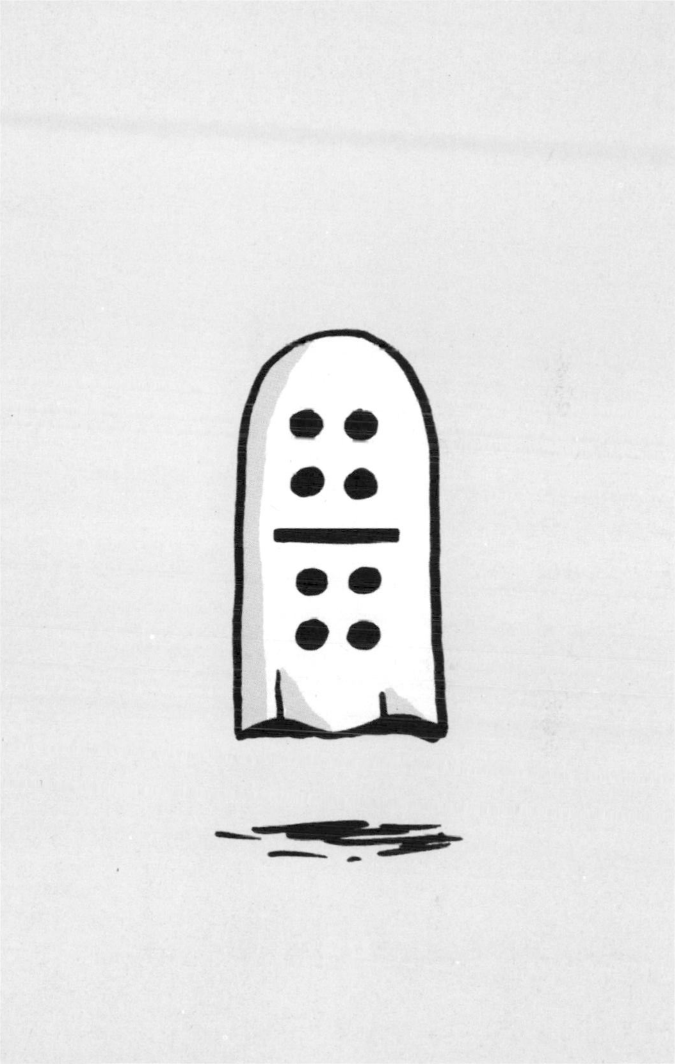

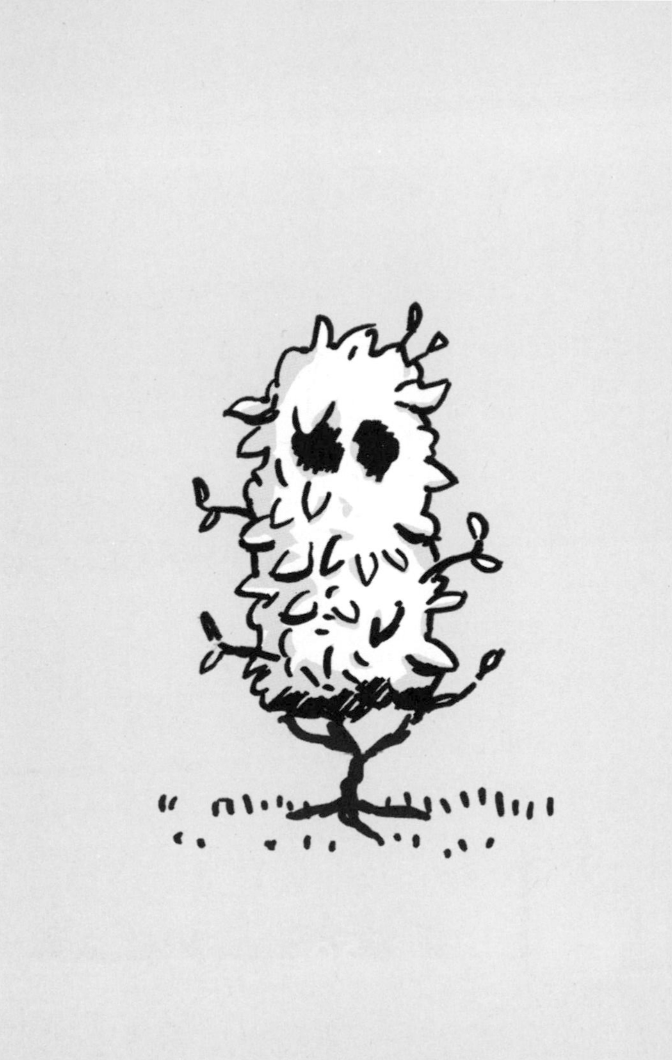

TOPIARY

50

NEARSIGHTED

51

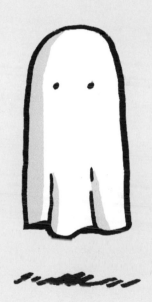

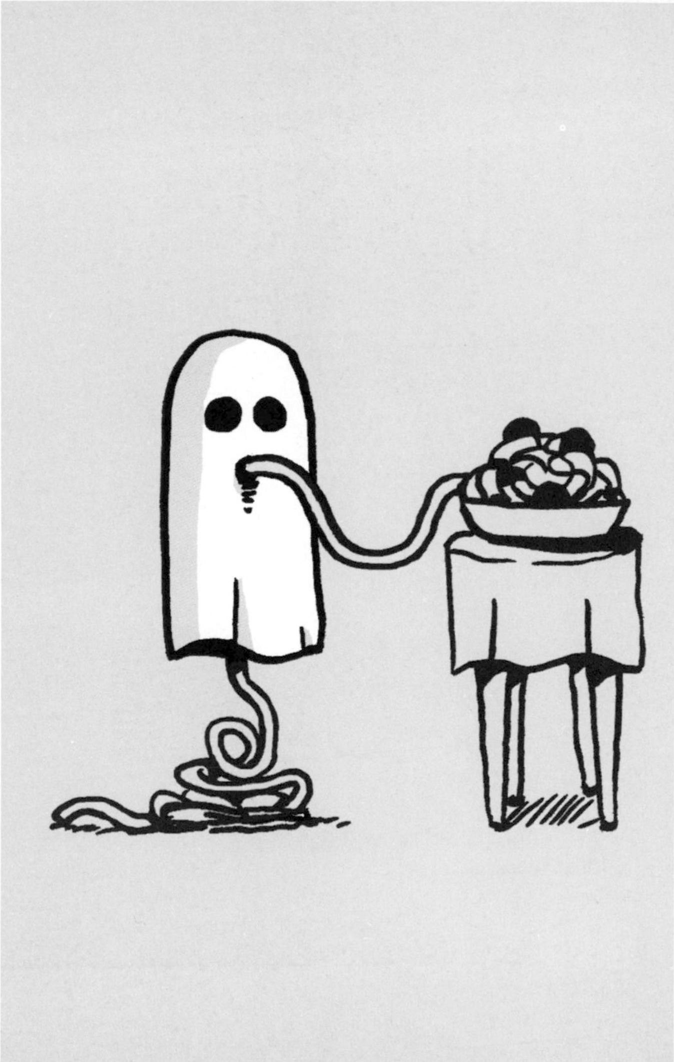

EATING
SPAGHETTI

52

MARSUPIAL

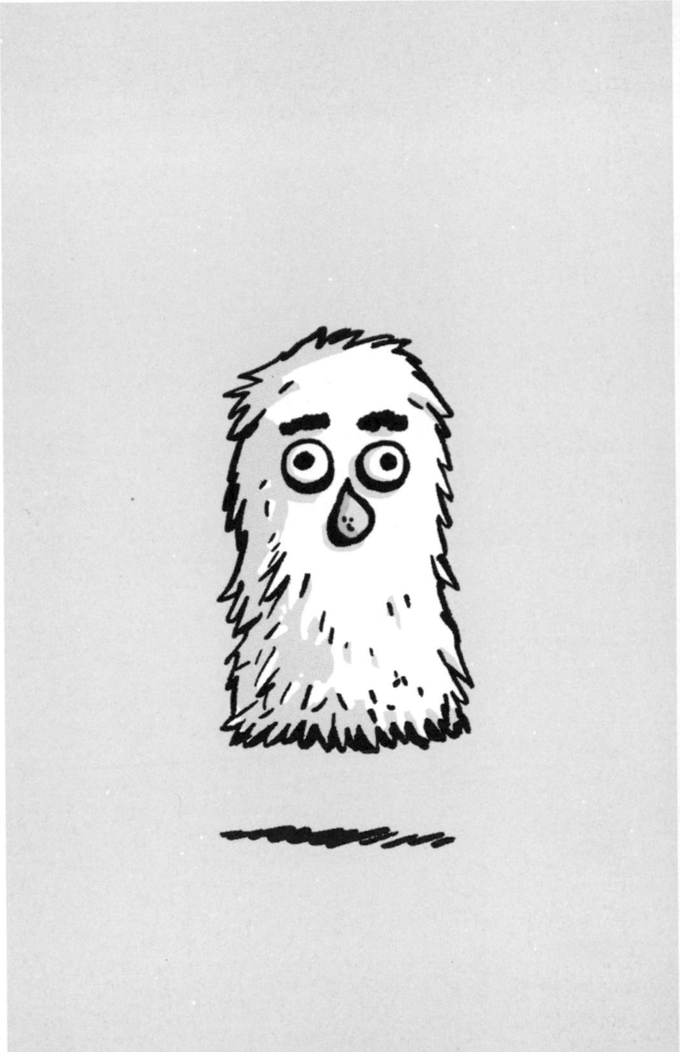

MUPPET

54

PEPPERONI

55

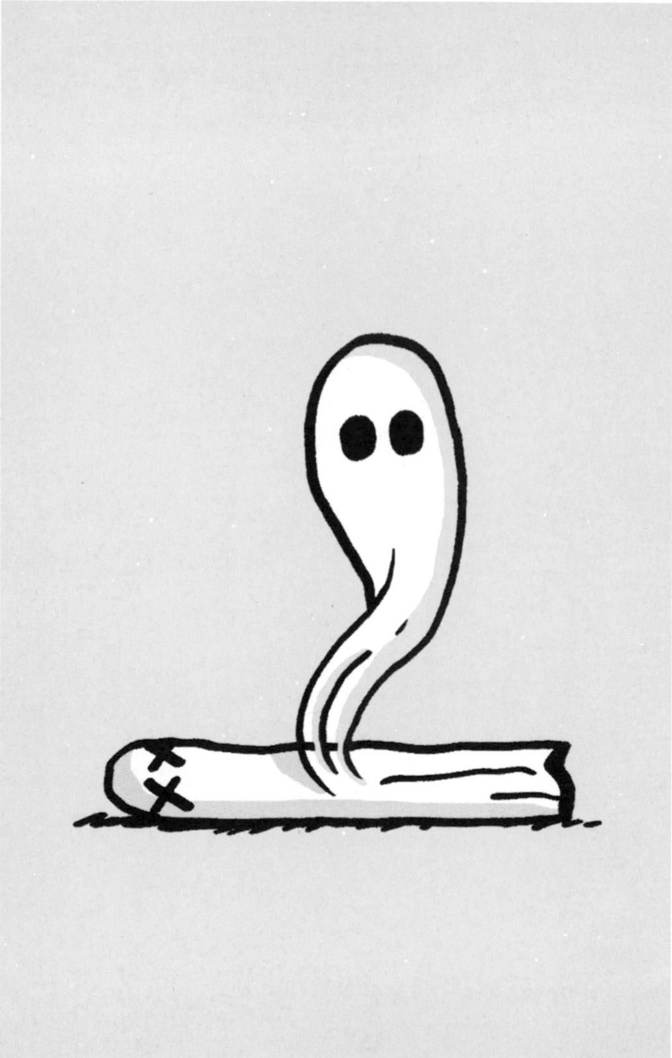

DEAD

56

GIANT ROBOT

57

JELLYFISH

58

PANDA

59

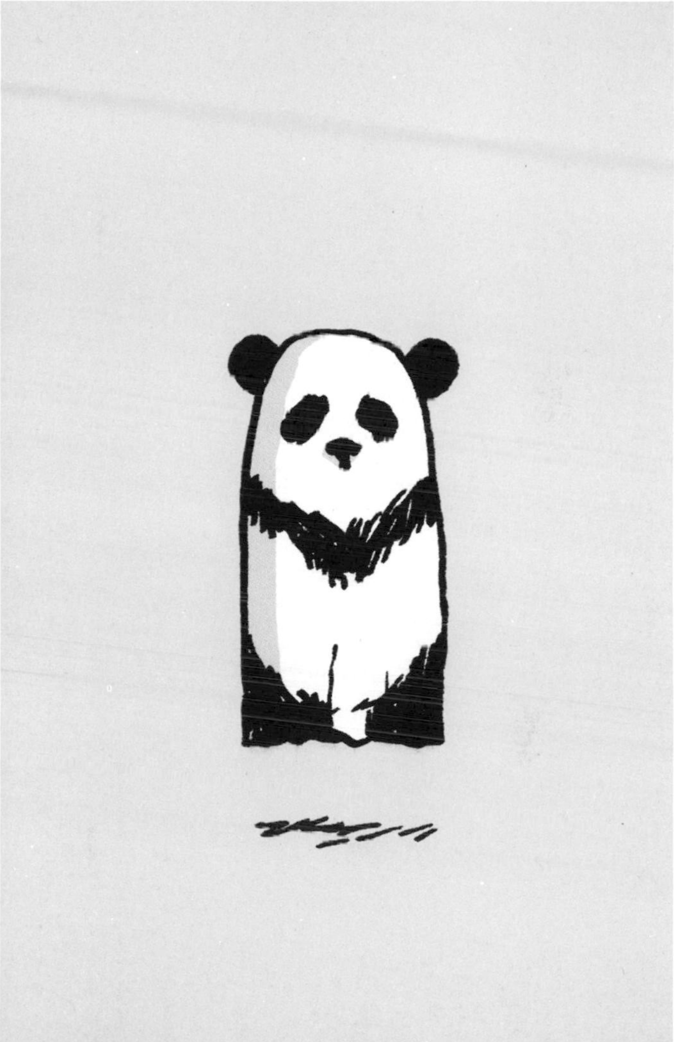

RUSSIAN
NESTING
GHOST

60

CLUMSY

61

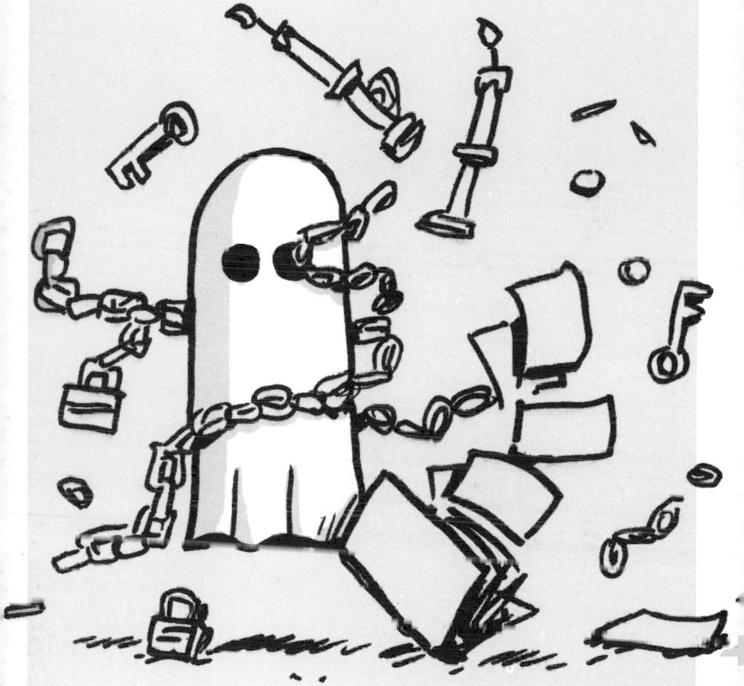

HIDEOUS
SKIRT

62

WORD

63

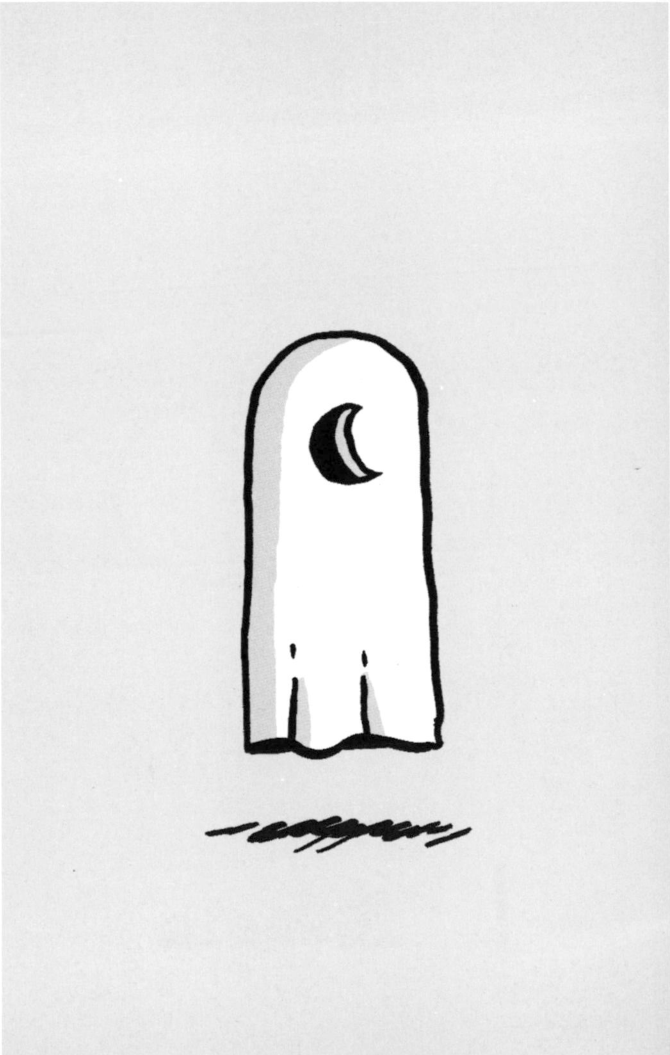

OUTHOUSE

64

HOCKEY MASK

65

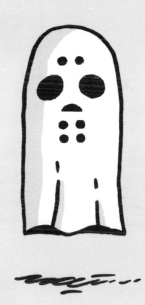

WITH CHERRY
ON TOP

IGLOO

67

PROP

68

THE BAD
CHINESE FOOD
YOU ATE
BEFORE BED

69

VENTRILOQUIST

70

OSTENTATIOUS

71

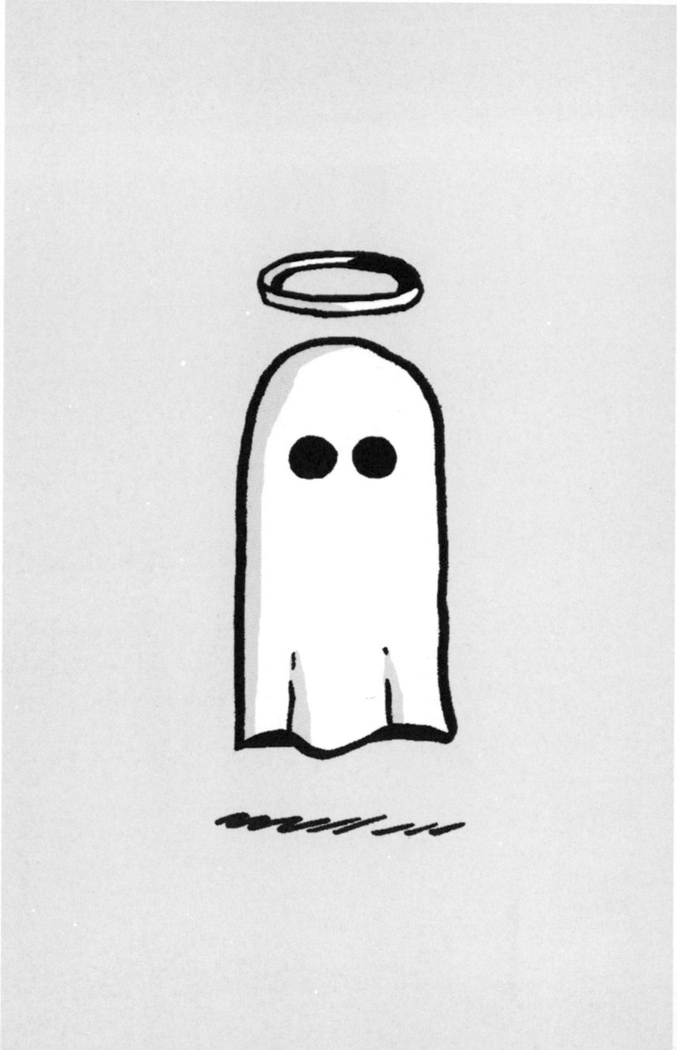

HOLY GHOST

72

SKULL

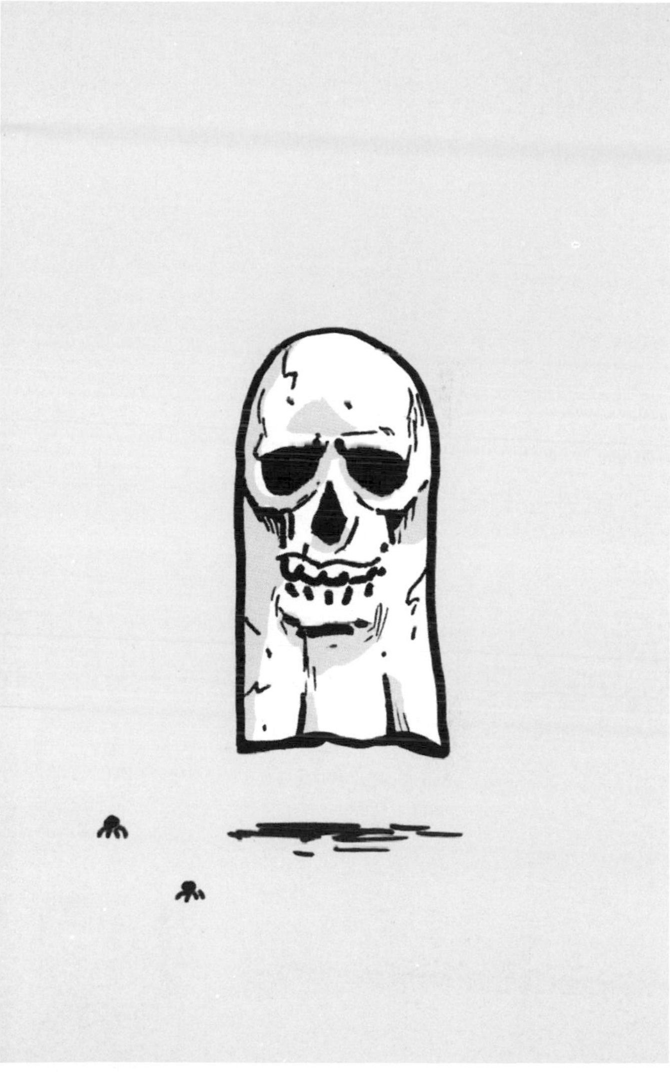

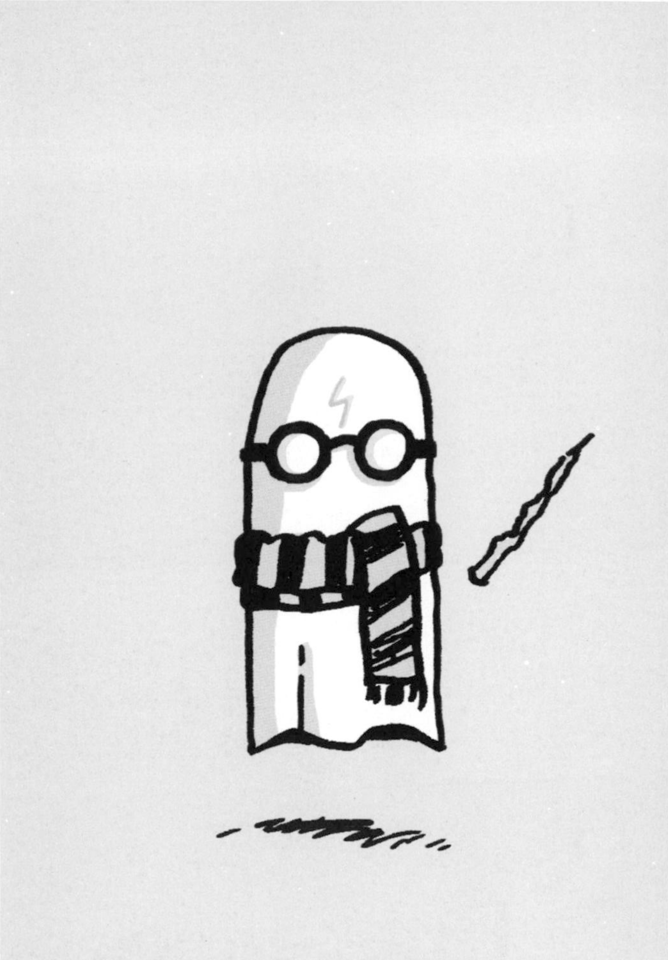

HARRY POTTER

74

GENIE

75

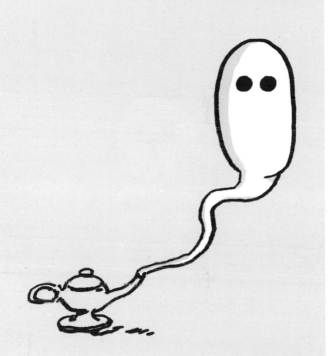

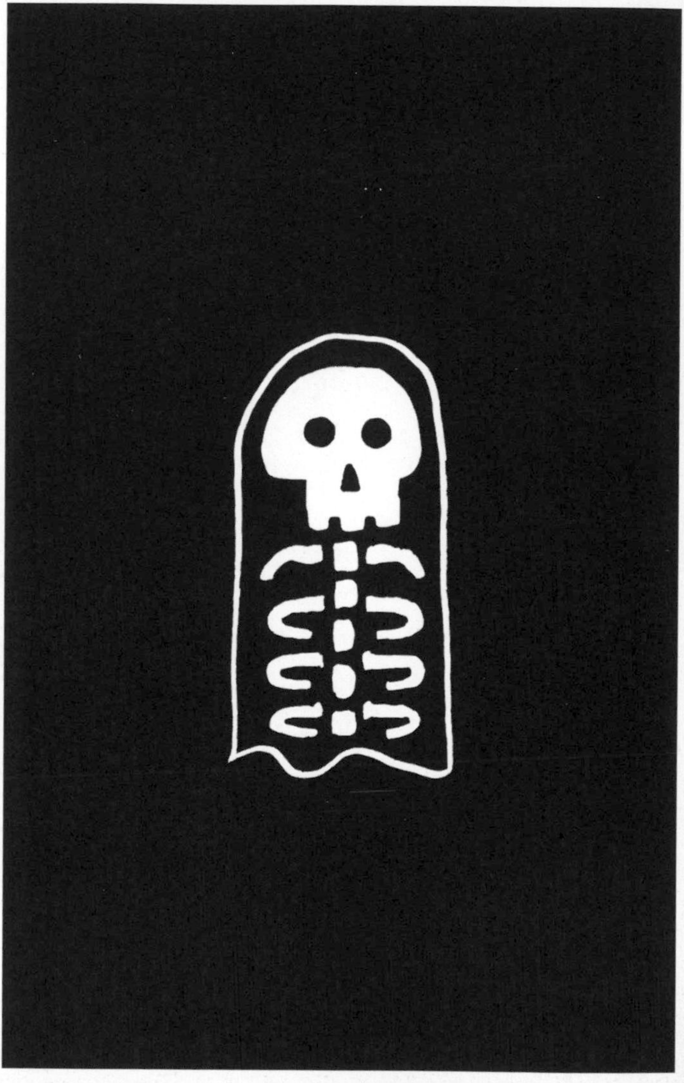

X-RAY

76

LUCHADOR

77

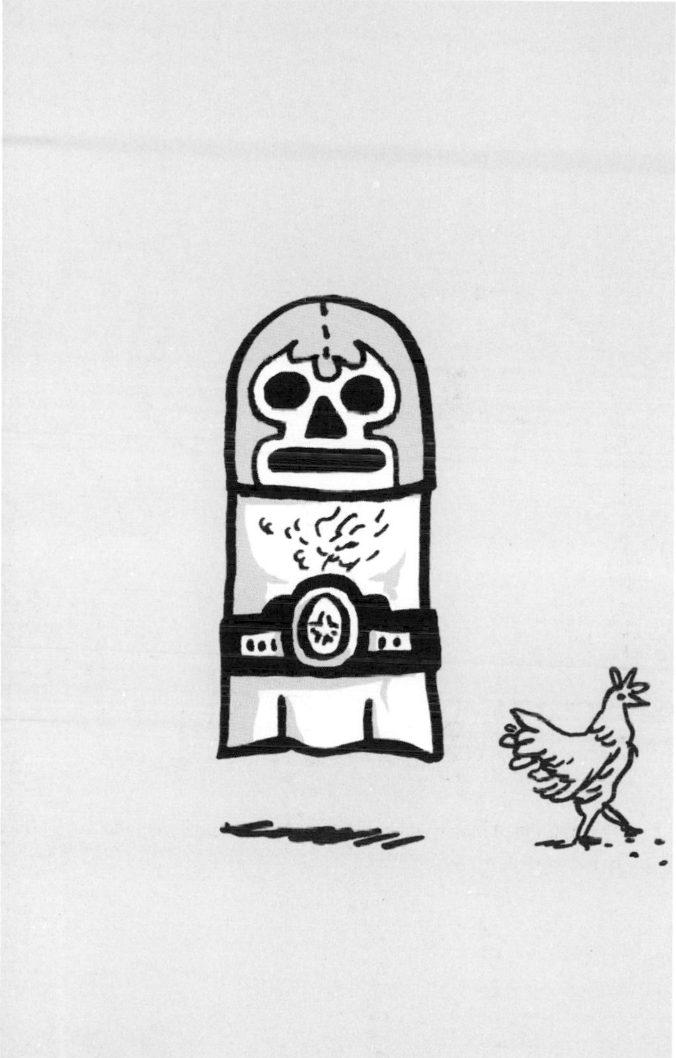

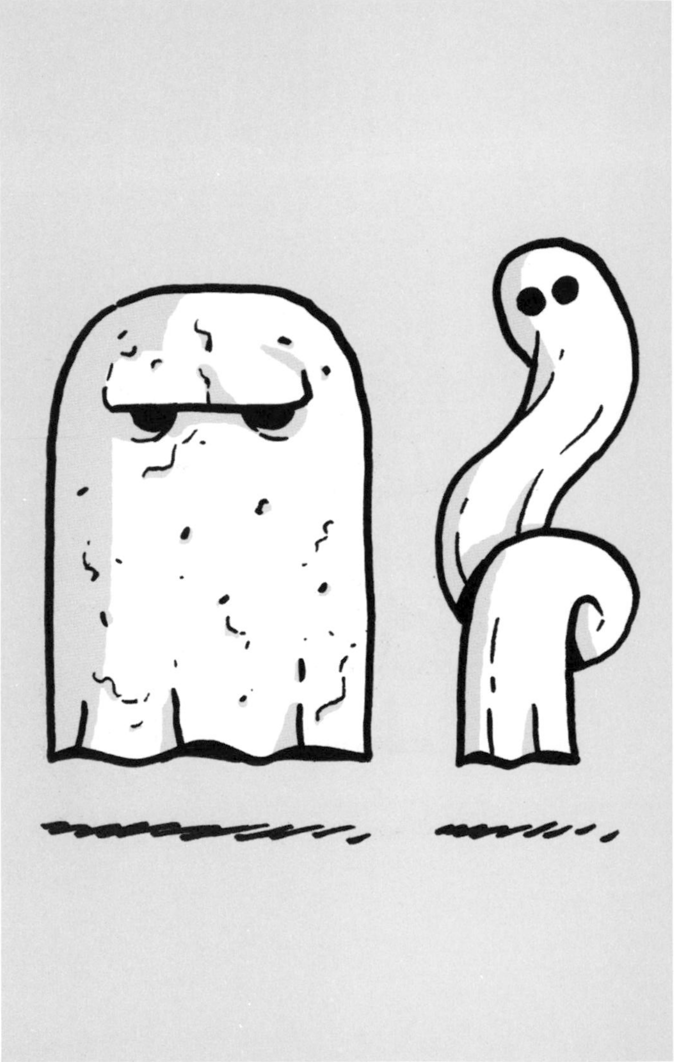

THE
FANTASTIC FOUR

POPSICLE

1
2
3
4
5
6
7 - 9

ROTATE 1 & 2 90° & SPREAD 1" APART.
CROWN WITH 3. ROTATE 4 90° & ALIGN
WITH TOPS OF 1 & 2, CENTERED HORIZONTALLY.
CONNECT EDGES OF 6 WITH BOTTOM OF 1 & 2.
PLACE 5 .25" BELOW 6. GARNISH 6 WITH
7-9. BOO!

SOME ASSEMBLY
REQUIRED

80

8-BIT

81

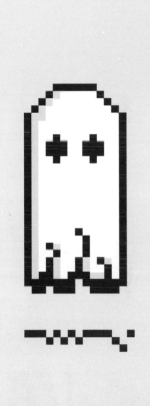

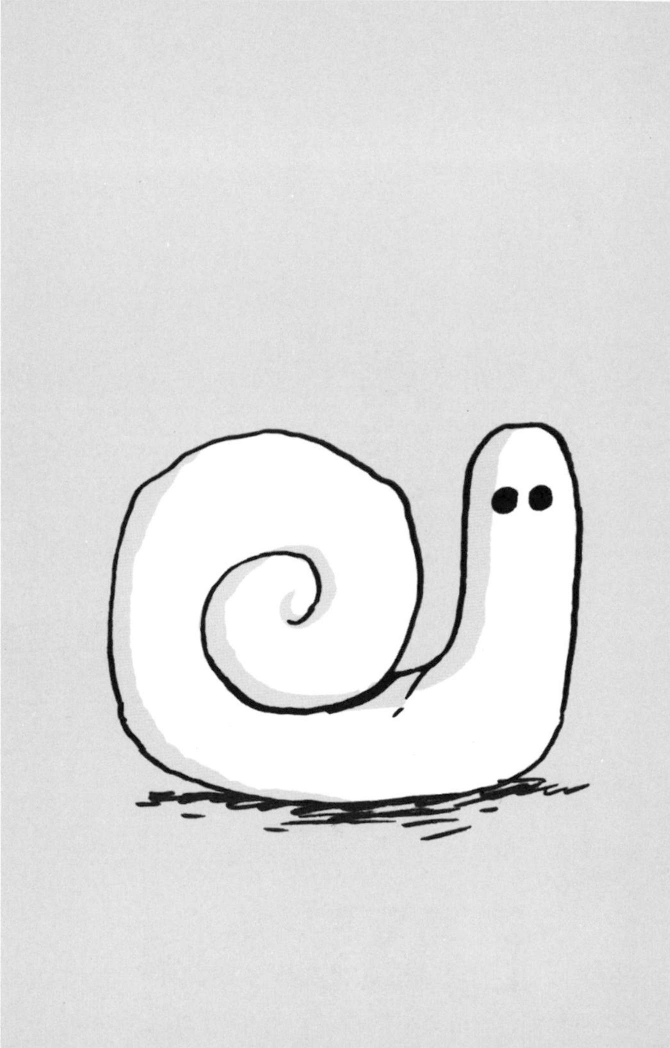

SNAIL

82

KINDERGARTEN

83

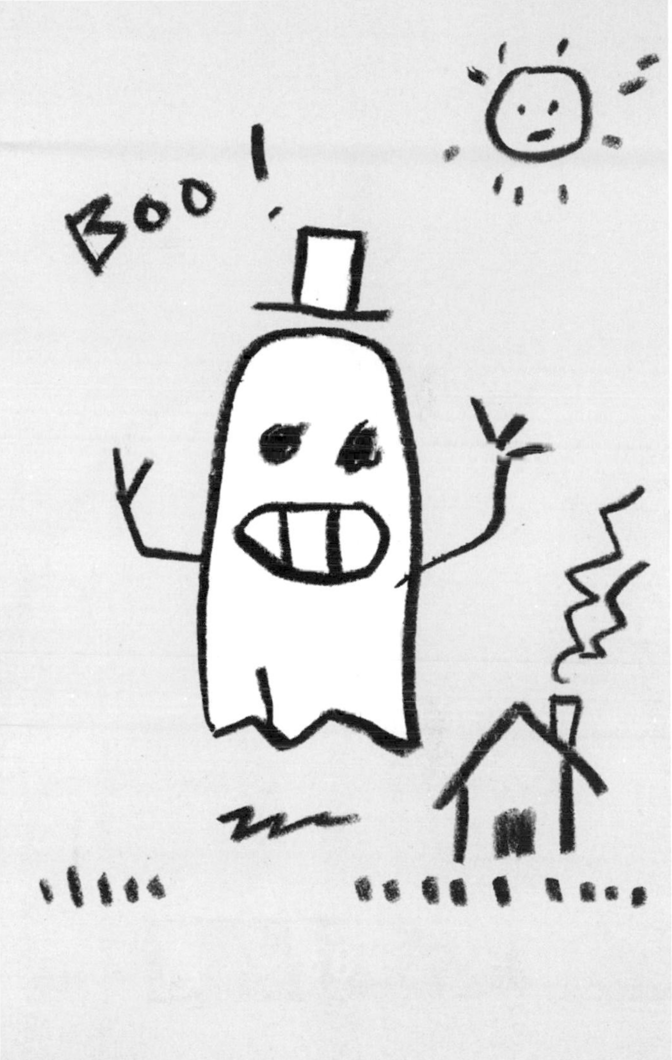
BOO!

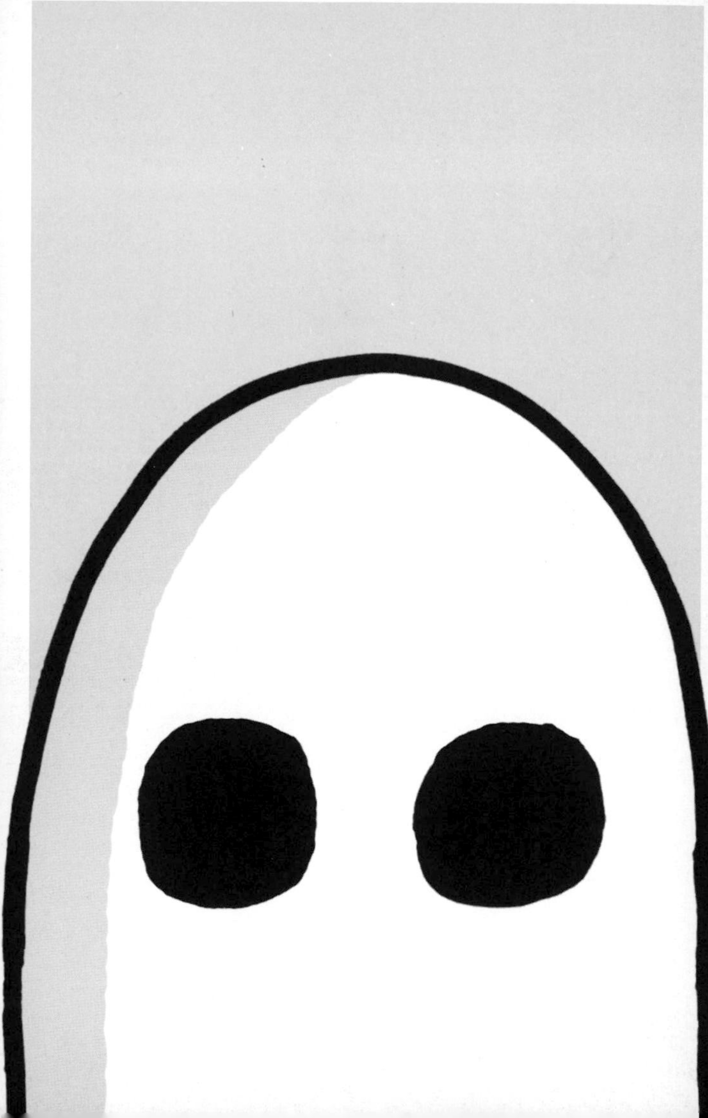

ALL UP IN
YOUR GRILL

84

VINYL

85

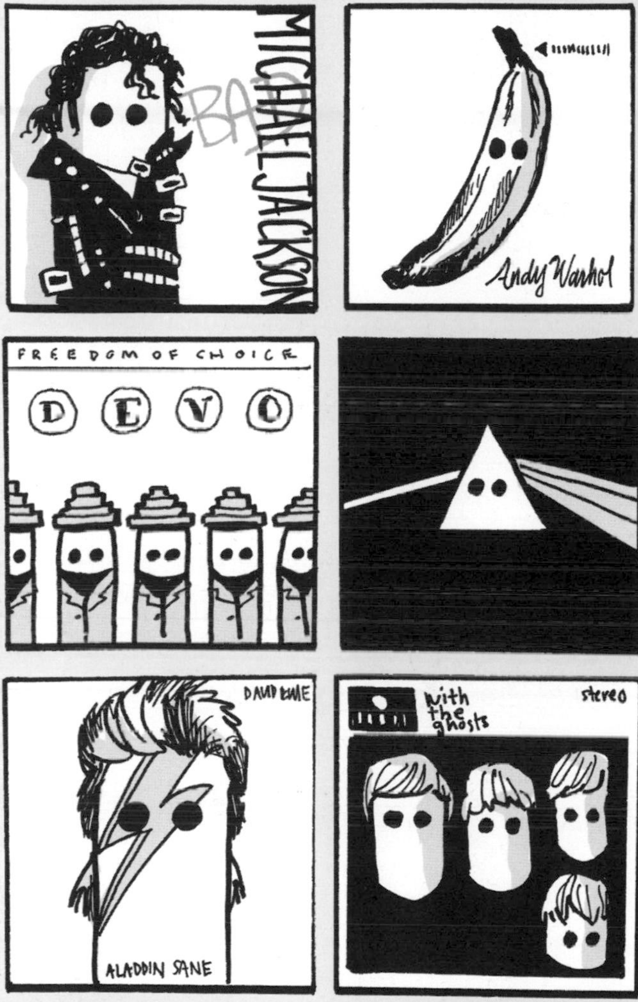
MICHAEL JACKSON
BAD
Andy Warhol
FREEDOM OF CHOICE
DEVO
ALADDIN SANE
with the ghosts
stereo

TERRYCLOTH

86

CHAMELEON

87

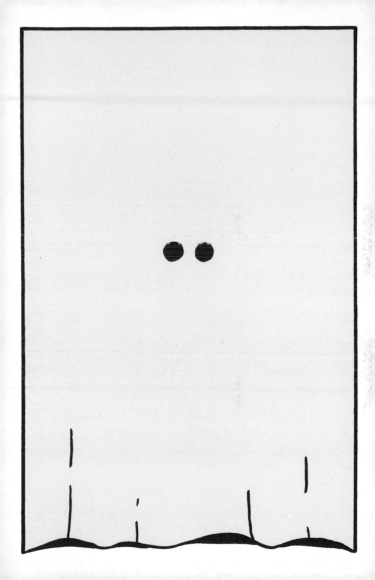

FILLED
WITH BEES

88

GRUMPY CAT

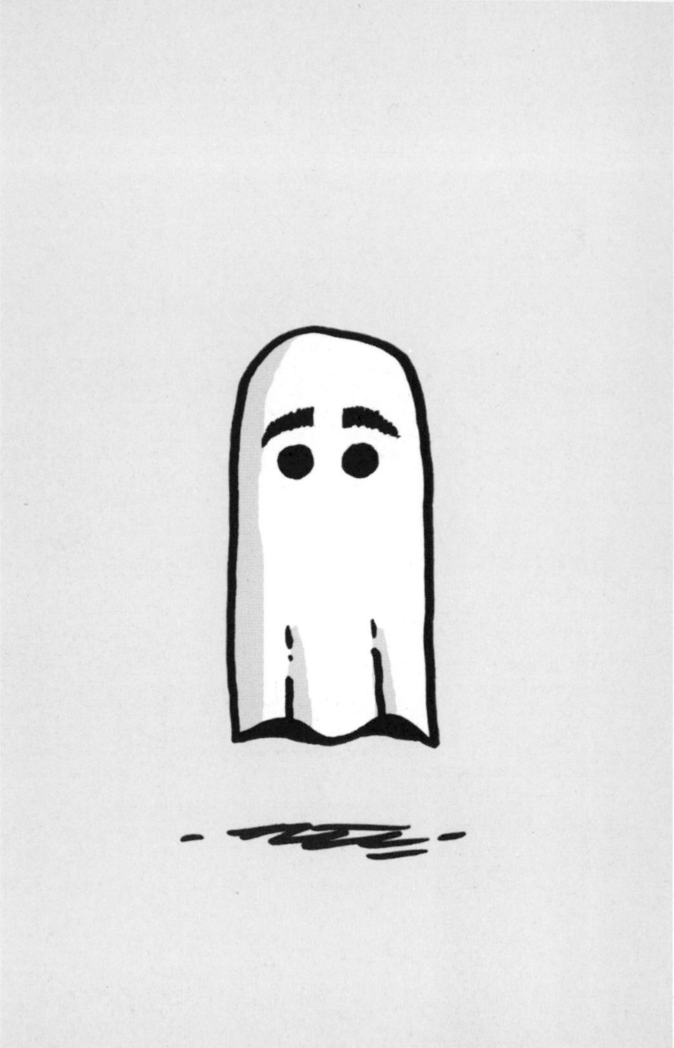

WITH EYEBROWS

90

RAINBOW
EYES

91

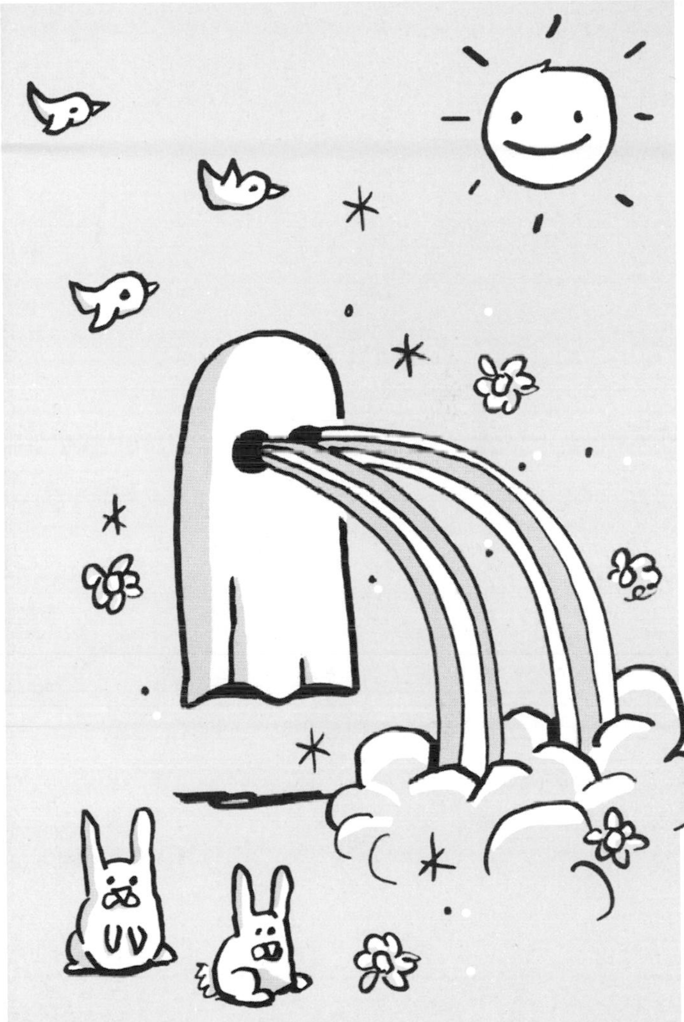

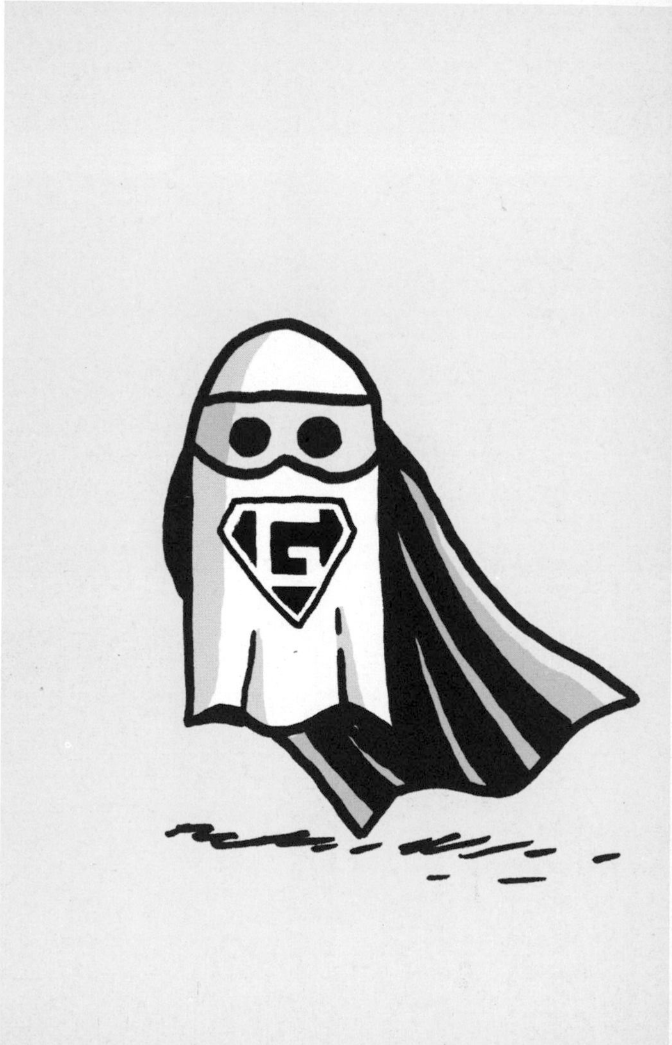

SUPERHERO

92

SKI MASK

93

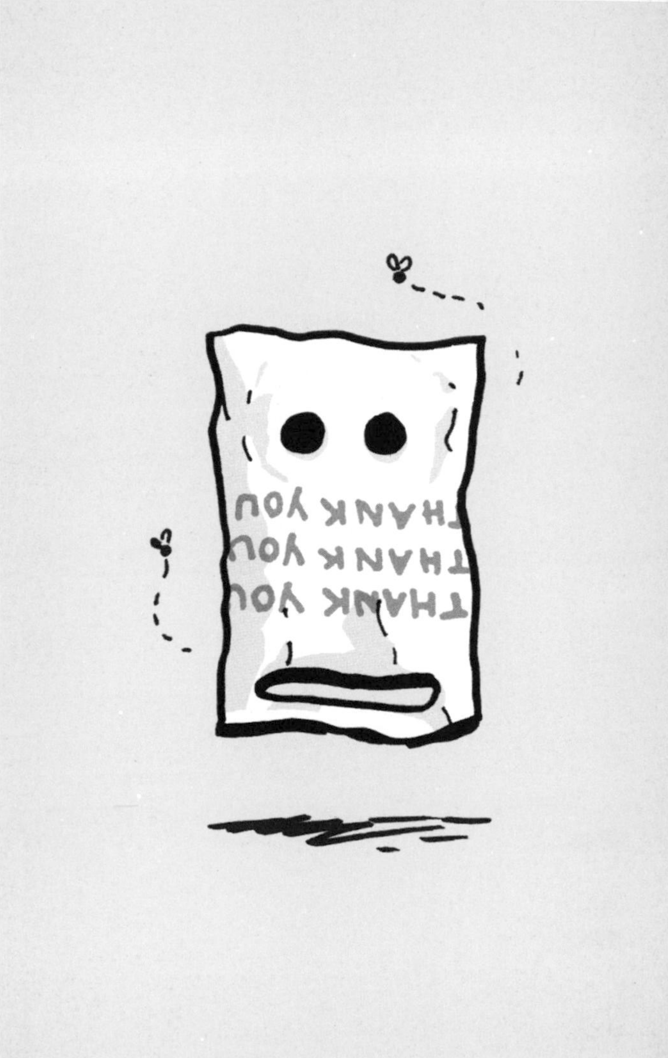
THANK YOU
THANK YOU
THANK YOU

SHOPPING
BAG

94

CACTUS

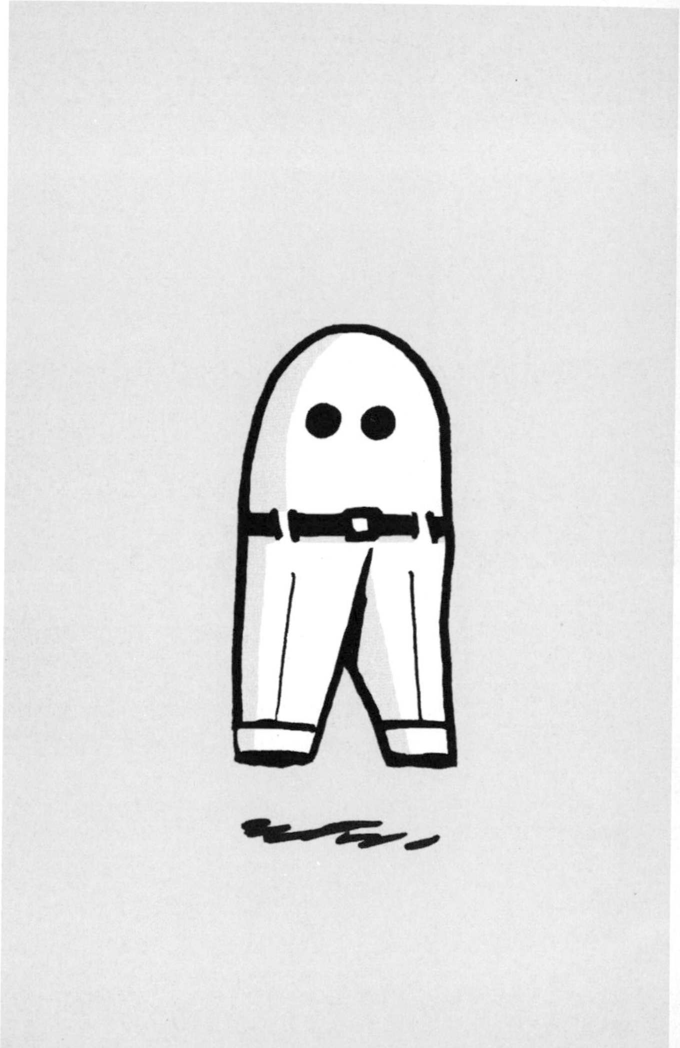

HAUNTED
CHINOS

96

USED CAR LOT

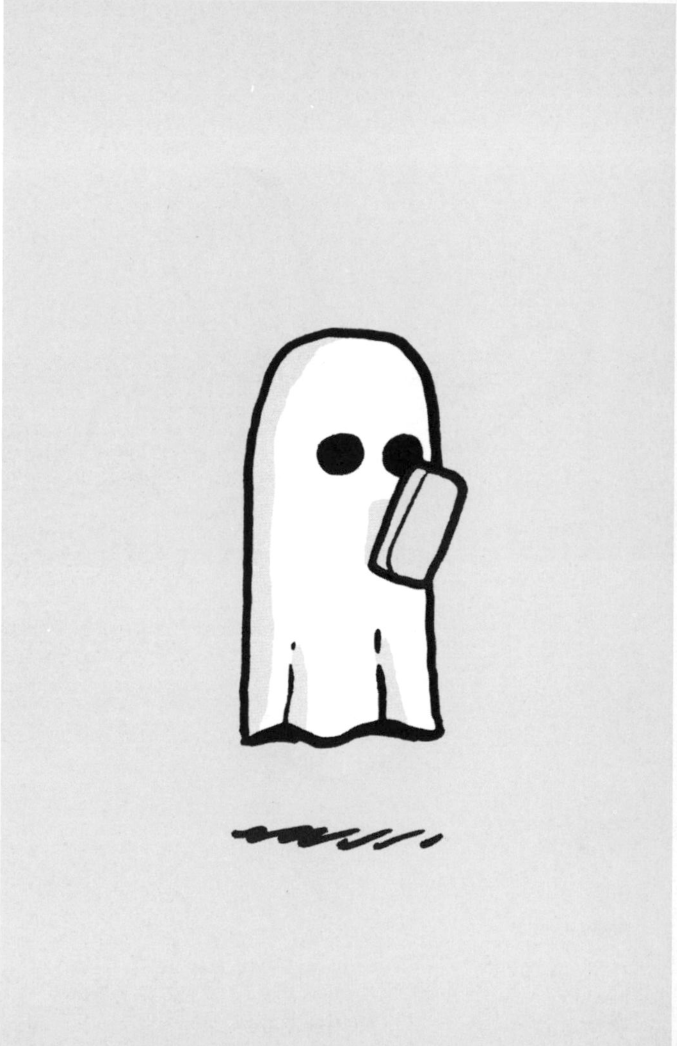

CHECKING
IPHONE

98

STEAMPUNK

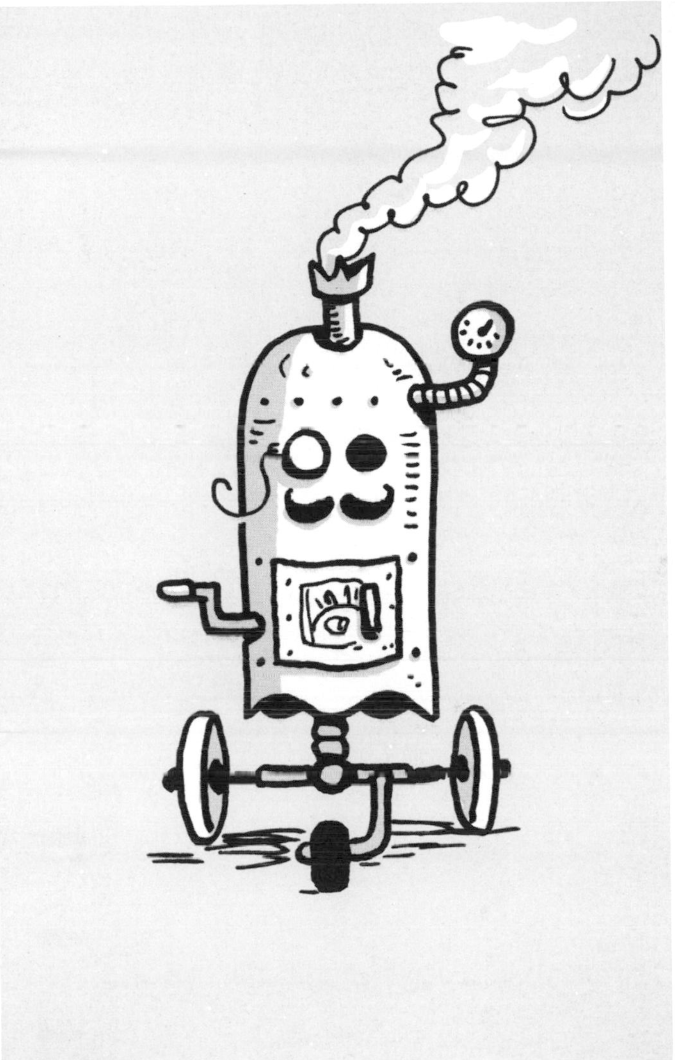

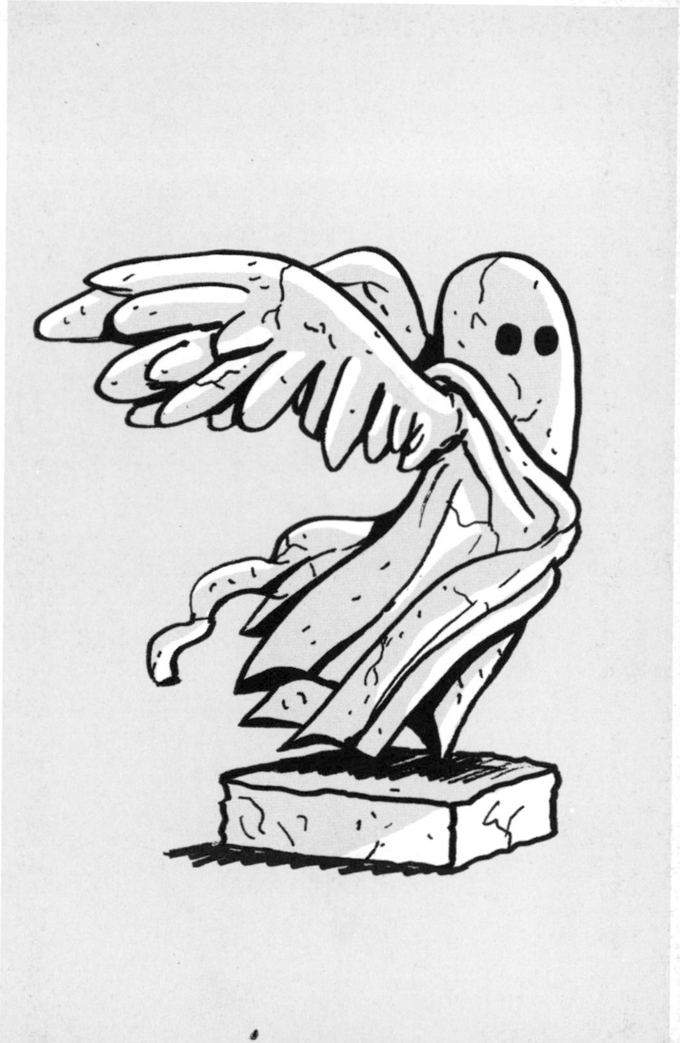